Test Bank

for

Press, Siever, Grotzinger, and Jordan's
Understanding Earth
Fourth Edition

SIMON M. PEACOCK
SONDRA S. PEACOCK

W. H. Freeman and Company
New York

Copyright © 2004 by W. H. Freeman and Company

Printed in the United States of America

ISBN: 0-7167-5784-2

First printing 2003

W. H. Freeman and Company
41 Madison Avenue
New York, NY 10010
Houndmills, Basingstoke RG21 6XS, England

Contents

Chapter 1: Building a Planet   1

Chapter 2: Plate Tectonics: The Unifying Theory   8

Chapter 3: Minerals: Building Blocks of Rocks   15

Chapter 4: Rocks: Records of Geologic Processes   23

Chapter 5: Igneous Rocks: Solids from Melts   31

Chapter 6: Volcanism   38

Chapter 7: Weathering and Erosion   45

Chapter 8: Sediments and Sedimentary Rocks   53

Chapter 9: Metamorphic Rocks   60

Chapter 10: The Rock Record and Geologic Time Scale   68

Chapter 11: Folds, Faults, and Other Records of Rock Deformation   76

Chapter 12: Mass Wasting   85

Chapter 13: The Hydrologic Cycle and Groundwater   93

Chapter 14: Rivers: Transport to the Oceans   102

Chapter 15: Winds and Deserts   111

Chapter 16: The Work of Ice   119

Chapter 17: Earth Beneath the Oceans   127

Chapter 18: Landscapes: Tectonic and Climate Interaction   135

Chapter 19: Earthquakes   143

Chapter 20: Evolution of the Continents   151

Chapter 21: Exploring Earth's Interior   160

Chapter 22: Energy and Material Resources from the Earth   167

Chapter 23: Earth's Environment, Global Change, and Human Impacts   176

Preface

From the Authors

As an aid in preparing introductory geology quizzes and exams, this *Test Bank* offers 1150 multiple-choice questions (50 questions per chapter) for the fourth edition of *Understanding Earth*. We have attempted to present a variety of different types of questions including geologic definitions (vocabulary), historical questions, concept questions, and practical questions. Each chapter contains sets of questions connected to geologic diagrams, such as cross sections. All of the questions in the test bank are tied directly to specific pages in the textbook. We encourage instructors to modify *Test Bank* questions and answers in order to incorporate topics and examples presented in their lectures that are not discussed in the textbook. Instructors should note that the wording of some *Test Bank* questions may provide answers or clues to other questions.

The *Graded Online Quizzes*, located at the Web site for the fourth edition of *Understanding Earth* (www.whfreeman.com/understandingearth) contain practice multiple-choice questions (20 questions per chapter) for students with built-in feedback. These quizzes are designed to help students better understand the material and prepare for exams. The vast majority of the online quiz questions are different than the test bank questions, although the questions cover similar concepts. **Test bank questions that are similar to online quiz questions are marked with an asterisk(*) in the test bank.** Instructors may wish to include these questions on their exams in order to encourage students to use the online quizzes. If desired, instructors could go one step further and incorporate online quiz questions directly into their exams.

In preparing this test bank, we have attempted to write clear, unambiguous questions based on our experience in preparing such exams over the 15 years. Despite our "experience," however, some of the questions that appear perfectly clear to us will strike students as unclear or ambiguous. We strongly encourage instructors to direct their students to choose the "best answer" to each question. If large numbers of students choose the same, incorrect answer to a question, then the instructor should scrutinize the question to see if the wording was confusing, and if so, modify the answer key or eliminate the question from the exam.

At many universities, introductory geology lectures involve presenting lectures to hundreds of students at a time. Because of large class sizes, exams commonly consist of multiple-choice questions graded by computer scanning. Nevertheless, in addition to multiple-choice questions, we strongly recommend that all introductory geology exams include one or two short essays to test and strengthen a student's ability to present their ideas clearly in writing. The essay grading burden can be significantly reduced by (1) grading essays on a coarse 0-2-4-6-8-10 point scale, so the instructor does not waste time worrying about differences involving one point, and (2) presenting examples of good essays in class. The latter technique frees the instructor from making detailed corrections on each essay and also demonstrates to students that they can say different things in different ways and still earn full credit for their essays.

Simon M. Peacock
Sondra S. Peacock
July 2003

Chapter 1: Building a Planet

1. Living organisms have been on Earth for _____ of Earth's history.
   A) less than 1%   B) about 20%   C) about 50%   D) about 80%
   Ans: D   Page: 1

2. Which of the following statements regarding the scientific method is <u>true</u>?
   A) A hypothesis must be agreed upon by more than one scientist.
   B) A theory is a hypothesis that has withstood many scientific tests.
   C) A theory is proven to be true, and therefore may not be discarded.
   D) A hypothesis cannot predict the outcome of scientific experiments.
   Ans: B   Page: 2

3. Which of the following statements about the scientific method is <u>false</u>?
   A) A scientific theory is never considered finally proved.
   B) Data used to generate a hypothesis may come from observations, experiments, and chance findings.
   C) A theory that has accumulated a substantial body of experimental support is called a hypothesis.
   D) A scientific model represents some aspect of nature based on a set of hypotheses and theories.
   Ans: C   Page: 2

4. What is a bolide?
   A) a dense solar nebula
   B) a large meteorite
   C) a lithospheric plate
   D) a molten volcanic projectile
   Ans: B   Page: 3

5. According to the principle of uniformitarianism, _____ .
   A) geologic processes we observe today have operated in the past
   B) animals evolved at a uniform rate
   C) all of the planets formed from a uniform solar nebula
   D) early Earth was covered by a uniform magma ocean
   Ans: A   Page: 3

6. When did the Big Bang take place?
   A) approximately 4.5 million years ago
   B) approximately 13 million years ago
   C) approximately 4.5 billion years ago
   D) approximately 13 billion years ago
   Ans: D   Page: 4

7. Why is the Sun's mass decreasing with time?
   A) because the temperature of the Sun is increasing
   B) because the Sun is contracting
   C) because the Sun's nuclear fusion consumes mass
   D) because the Sun's volume is increasing
   Ans: C   Page: 5

8. Under intense pressure and high temperature, hydrogen atoms combine to form helium. This process is called _____.
   A) convection   B) metamorphism   C) nuclear fission   D) nuclear fusion
   Ans: D   Page: 5

9. According to the nebular hypothesis, the inner planets are dense and rocky because _____ .
   A) the inner planets were the first to condense from the solar nebula.
   B) the lighter gases were blown away by the Sun's radiation.
   C) heavy elements were created by fusion within the inner planets.
   D) the inner planets' gravitational pull attracted dense material from the outer planets.
   Ans: B   Page: 5

10. What caused dust and condensing material to accrete into planetesimals?
    A) gravitational attraction and collisions   C) nuclear fusion
    B) heating of gases   D) rotation of the proto-sun
    Ans: A   Page: 5

11. The four inner planets are _____.
    A) mostly hot, with heavy, dense, atmospheres.
    B) all similar to the Earth in size, atmosphere, and density.
    C) larger and less dense than the outer planets.
    D) small, rocky, and relatively lacking in volatile elements.
    Ans: D   Page: 5

12. Nebulae are composed primarily of which of the following elements?
    A) hydrogen and helium   C) iron and silicon
    B) hydrogen and oxygen   D) oxygen and silicon
    Ans: A   Page: 5

13. Which of the following is not one of the giant outer planets?
    A) Neptune   B) Uranus   C) Saturn   D) Venus
    Ans: D   Page: 6

14. The giant outer planets are composed mostly of _____.
    A) carbon dioxide   C) oxygen and nitrogen
    B) hydrogen and helium   D) rocks and ice
    Ans: B   Page: 6

15. How old is the Earth?
    A) approximately 4.5 thousand years old   C) approximately 4.5 billion years old
    B) approximately 4.5 million years old   D) approximately 4.5 trillion years old
    Ans: C   Page: 7

16. What is the process by which an originally homogeneous Earth developed a dense core and a light crust?
    A) accretion   B) compression   C) differentiation   D) metamorphism
    Ans: C   Page: 7

17. The heat that caused melting in Earth's early history was supplied from which of the following events or causes?
    A) volcanic activity and radioactivity   C) a large impact event and radioactivity
    B) solar heating and volcanic activity   D) a large impact event and solar heating
    Ans: C   Page: 7

18. The Earth's core is made up primarily of _____ .
    A) iron   B) lead   C) oxygen   D) silicon
    Ans: A   Alternative Location: Online quizzing   Page: 7

Use the following to answer question 19:

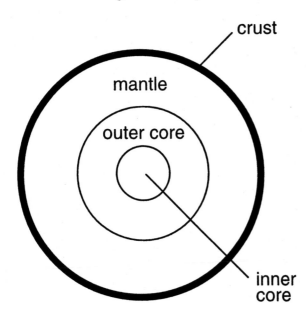

19. Which part of the Earth depicted in the figure above is molten?
    A) crust   B) mantle   C) outer core   D) inner core
    Ans: C   Page: 7

20. Which of the following statements about the age of the Earth and Moon is <u>true</u>?
    A) The Earth is approximately 3 billion years older than the Moon.
    B) The Earth and Moon are approximately the same age.
    C) The Earth is approximately 1.5 billion years younger than the Moon.
    D) The Earth is approximately 4.5 billion years younger than the Moon.
    Ans: B   Page: 7

21. Bolide impacts are generally thought to be responsible for all of the following <u>except</u>:
    A) differentiation of Earth's crust, mantle, and core
    B) extinction of the dinosaurs
    C) formation of the Moon
    D) formation of Meteor Crater (Arizona)
    Ans: A   Page: 7

22. Which of the following elements is more abundant in the Earth's crust as compared to the Earth as a whole?
    A) iron   B) magnesium   C) nickel   D) silicon
    Ans: D   Page: 8

23. Which of the following makes up the bulk of the Earth?
    A) crust   B) inner core   C) mantle   D) outer core
    Ans: C   Page: 8

24. Ninety percent of the Earth is made up of which four elements?
    A) iron, oxygen, silicon, and magnesium
    B) oxygen, nitrogen, hydrogen, and silicon
    C) magnesium, aluminum, silicon, and oxygen
    D) silicon, calcium, aluminum, and iron
    Ans: A   Page: 8

25. Approximately 50% of the Earth's crust is made up of which element?
    A) aluminum   B) iron   C) oxygen   D) silicon
    Ans: C   Page: 8

26. How did Earth develop an oxygen-rich atmosphere?
    A) The Earth was bombarded by oxygen-rich comets.
    B) Photosynthesis released oxygen, which accumulated gradually.
    C) Sunlight broke water down to form oxygen and hydrogen.
    D) The weathering of rocks released oxygen.
    Ans: B   Page: 9

27. Which of the following planets is <u>not</u> geologically active?
    A) Earth   B) Mars   C) Mercury   D) Venus
    Ans: C   Page: 9

28. The evidence that Mars once had water includes _____.
    A) dry river beds and valleys.
    B) large salt deposits from dried-up oceans.
    C) liquid water in current Martian oceans.
    D) water vapor in the Martian atmosphere.
    Ans: A   Page: 10

29. Which of the following statements about Mars is <u>false</u>?
    A) Mars has a thin, cold atmosphere.
    B) Mars has networks of valleys and dry river channels.
    C) Mars has liquid water and a corrosive atmosphere.
    D) Mars has a land surface much older than that of the Earth.
    Ans: C   Page: 10

30. Which of the following solar system bodies is <u>least</u> likely to have water ice on its surface?
    A) Earth   B) Mars   C) Moon   D) Venus
    Ans: D   Page: 10

31. The Earth exchanges _____ with the rest of the cosmos.
    A) energy and mass
    B) energy, but not mass,
    C) mass, but not energy,
    D) neither energy nor mass
    Ans: A   Page: 12

32. Solar energy energizes all of the following major components of the Earth system <u>except</u> the _____.
    A) atmosphere   B) biosphere   C) hydrosphere   D) lithosphere
    Ans: D   Page: 12

33. What powers the Earth's external heat engine?
    A) gravitational energy   B) radioactive decay   C) solar energy   D) tidal forces
    Ans: C   Page: 12

34. Which of the following powers the Earth's internal heat engine?
    A) radioactivity
    B) heat trapped during the formation of the Earth
    C) A and B
    D) neither A nor B
    Ans: C   Page: 12

35. In which of the following subsystems is the Earth's magnetic field generated?
    A) climate system
    B) geodynamo system
    C) hydrologic system
    D) plate tectonic system
    Ans: B   Page: 14

36. Earth's climate system involves interactions between the atmosphere and the
    _____.
    A) biosphere
    B) hydrosphere
    C) lithosphere
    D) biosphere, hydrosphere, and lithosphere
    Ans: D   Page: 14

37. On average, Earth's lithosphere is approximately ____ km thick.
    A) 4   B) 20   C) 100   D) 500
    Ans: C   Page: 14

38. The asthenosphere is _____.
    A) cool and strong   B) cool and weak   C) hot and strong   D) hot and weak
    Ans: D   Page: 14

39. What are the "plates" of plate tectonics made up of?
    A) asthenosphere   B) crust   C) lithosphere   D) mantle
    Ans: C   Page: 14

40. Which of the following relationships is correct?
    A) asthenosphere = crust   C) lithosphere = crust
    B) asthenosphere = crust + upper mantle   D) lithosphere = crust + upper mantle
    Ans: D   Page: 14

41. The motion of a flowing material where hot matter rises from the bottom and cool
    matter sinks from the surface is called _____ .
    A) accretion   B) convection   C) differentiation   D) fusion
    Ans: B   Page: 15

42. Which of the following statements about convection is true?
    A) Heat is transferred from hot material to cool material without inducing a flow.
    B) Hot material flows upward and displaces cool material.
    C) Cool material flows upward and displaces hot material.
    D) Random circulation occurs.
    Ans: B   Page: 15

43. How old are the oldest rocks now found on the Earth's surface?
    A) 0.5 billion years old   C) 4.0 billion years old
    B) 2.5 billion years old   D) 4.5 billion years old
    Ans: C   Page: 16

44. Earth's atmosphere has been oxygen-rich for _____ of Earth's history.
    A) about 25%   B) about 50%   C) about 75%   D) about 99%
    Ans: B   Page: 16

45. Large continental masses had formed on Earth by _____.
    A) 0.3 billion years ago   C) 2.5 billion years ago
    B) 1.0 billion years ago   D) 4.0 billion years ago
    Ans: C   Page: 16

46. Which of the following pieces of geologic evidence is used to date when the Earth's atmosphere became oxygen rich?
    A) the oldest fossils of flowering plants
    B) the oldest fossils of primitive bacteria
    C) the oldest rocks showing evidence of erosion by water
    D) the oldest rusted iron-bearing rocks
    Ans: D   Page: 17

47. How old are the earliest fossil remains?
    A) about 65 million years old   C) about 2200 million years old
    B) about 540 million years old   D) about 3500 million years old
    Ans: D   Page: 17

48. Which two of the following compounds are the products of photosynthesis?
    I.   carbohydrates
    II.   carbon dioxide
    III.   oxygen
    IV.   water
    A) I and III   B) II and IV   C) I and IV   D) II and III
    Ans: A   Page: 17

49. When did biology's "Big Bang" (evolutionary explosion) occur?
    A) about 65 million years ago   C) about 2200 million years ago
    B) about 540 million years ago   D) about 3500 million years ago
    Ans: B   Page: 18

50. What caused the mass extinctions 65 million years ago that ended the Age of Dinosaurs?
    A) major bolide impact   C) massive volcanic eruptions
    B) global glaciation   D) all of the above
    Ans: A   Page: 18

Chapter 2: Plate Tectonics: The Unifying Theory

1. Who proposed the theory of continental drift?
   A) Charles Darwin   B) Harry Hess   C) Alfred Wegener   D) J. Tuzo Wilson
   Ans: C   Page: 24

2. Which of the following concepts was developed earliest?
   A) continental drift
   B) plate tectonics
   C) sea-floor spreading
   D) All three concepts were developed at about the same time.
   Ans: A   Page: 24

3. What age are the fossils of the reptile *Mesosaurus* found in Africa and South America
   that suggest the two continents were once together?
   A) about 100 million years old   C) about 1000 million years old
   B) about 300 million years old   D) about 3000 million years old
   Ans: B   Page: 25

4. When was the theory of plate tectonics developed?
   A) 1860s   B) 1920s   C) 1940s   D) 1960s
   Ans: D   Page: 26

   Use the following to answer questions 5-8:

   Use the following possible answers for the questions below.
   I.   convergent plate boundaries
   II.   divergent plate boundaries
   III. transform fault boundaries

5. Where is new lithosphere created?
   A) I   B) II   C) III   D) I and II
   Ans: B   Alternative Location: Online quizzing   Page: 27

6. Where does volcanism occur?
   A) I   B) I and II   C) II and III   D) I, II, and III
   Ans: B   Page: 30-32

7. Where are the world's highest mountain ranges created?
   A) I   B) I and II   C) II and III   D) I, II, and III
   Ans: A   Page: 33

8. Which type(s) of plate boundaries indicate(s) the direction of relative plate motions?
   A) I   B) II   C) III   D) I, II, and III
   Ans: C   Page: 41

9. New lithosphere is created _____.
   A) in deep sea trenches   C) in subduction zones
   B) at mid-ocean ridges   D) along transform faults
   Ans: B   Page: 30

Use the following to answer questions 10-11:

The following refer to the cross section of plate boundary depicted below:

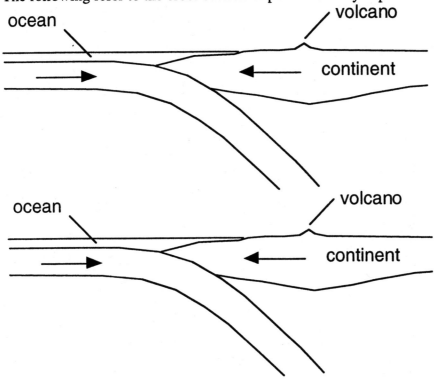

10. What type of plate boundary is shown in the diagram?
    A) a continent collision   C) a subduction zone
    B) a spreading center   D) a transform fault
    Ans: C   Page: 31

11. Which of the following locations could be represented by the diagram?
    A) the east coast of Africa   C) the west coast of South America
    B) the east coast of North America   D) the west coast of Europe
    Ans: C   Page: 32

12. In which ocean are most of the world's convergent plate margins located?
    A) Arctic Ocean   B) Atlantic Ocean   C) Indian Ocean   D) Pacific Ocean
    Ans: D   Page: 31-32

13. The east coast of North America is _____.
    A) a convergent plate boundary   C) a transform plate boundary
    B) a divergent plate boundary   D) not a plate boundary
    Ans: D   Page: 29

14. Which of the following is associated with a divergent plate boundary?
    A) earthquakes   B) volcanism   C) rifting   D) all of the above
    Ans: D   Page: 30

15. Which of the following is a divergent plate boundary?
    A) the Andes Mountains   C) the Mid-Atlantic Ridge
    B) the Himalayan Mountains   D) the San Andreas Fault
    Ans: C   Page: 30

16. At what type of plate boundary do the deepest earthquakes occur?
    A) convergent
    B) divergent
    C) transform
    D) All of these plate boundaries have deep earthquakes.
    Ans: A   Page: 31

17. Approximately how deep (below sea level) are the deepest deep-sea trenches?
    A) 3 km   B) 10 km   C) 30 km   D) 100 km
    Ans: B   Page: 31

18. Which of the following is not associated with convergent plate boundaries?
    A) earthquakes   B) deep-sea trenches   C) spreading centers   D) volcanoes
    Ans: C   Page: 31

19. Which of the following is a type of convergent plate boundary?
    A) continental rift   B) mid-ocean ridge   C) spreading center   D) subduction zone
    Ans: D   Page: 31

20. Which of the following mountain ranges formed as a result of ocean-continent convergence?
    A) the Andes   B) the Appalachians   C) the Himalayas   D) the Urals
    Ans: A   Page: 32

21. When a deep-sea trench is located next to a continent, where would you expect to find active volcanoes?
    A) on the ocean side of the trench
    B) in the deep-sea trench
    C) on the continent side of the trench
    D) on both the ocean side and continent side of the trench
    Ans: C   Page: 32

22. What plate is subducting beneath southwestern Canada and the northwestern United States?
    A) the Cocos plate   C) the Nazca plate
    B) the Juan de Fuca plate   D) the Pacific plate
    Ans: B   Page: 32

23. The west coast of South America is _____.
    A) a convergent plate boundary   C) a transform fault boundary
    B) a divergent plate boundary   D) not a plate boundary
    Ans: A   Page: 32

24. Which of the following is an example of a transform plate boundary?
    A) the East African Rift   C) the Mid-Atlantic Ridge
    B) the Marianas Trench   D) the San Andreas Fault
    Ans: D   Page: 32

25. What type of plate boundary is parallel to the direction of plate movement?
    A) convergent plate boundaries   C) transform plate boundaries
    B) divergent plate boundaries   D) all of the above
    Ans: C   Page: 32

26. Which of the following mountain ranges is the product of continent-continent convergence?
    A) Andes   B) Cascade Range   C) Himalayas   D) Japanese Islands
    Ans: C   Page: 32

27. The North American plate is bounded by _____ plate boundaries.
    A) convergent   C) transform
    B) divergent   D) convergent, divergent, and transform
    Ans: D   Page: 34

28. Which of the following can be used to determine the rates of plate motion?
    A) astronomical positioning   C) seafloor magnetic anomalies
    B) global positioning system   D) all of the above
    Ans: D   Page: 34-40

Use the following to answer questions 29-30:

The following questions refer to the cross section below which depicts magnetized oceanic crust at a spreading center. The "+" symbol indicates positive (normal) magnetic anomalies; the "–" symbol indicates negative (reversed) magnetic anomalies.

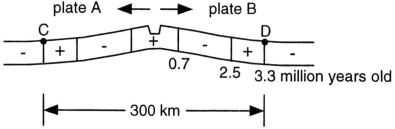

29. How fast are points C and D spreading apart from each other?
    A) about 20 millimeters/year   C) about 100 millimeters/year
    B) about 50 millimeters/year   D) about 200 millimeters/year
    Ans: C   Page: 35

30. "Normal" magnetized crust at the spreading center formed during the _____ epoch.
    A) Brunhes   B) Gauss   C) Gilbert   D) Matuyama
    Ans: A   Page: 35

31. Modern seafloor spreading rates range from _____.
    A) 0.2 to 1.5 millimeters per year   C) 2 to 15 meters per year
    B) 2 to 15 centimeters per year   D) 2 to 15 kilometers per year
    Ans: B   Page: 36

32. What two scientists related the positive and negative magnetic bands on the seafloor to seafloor spreading?
    A) Charles Darwin and James Hutton   C) F.J. Vine and D.H. Mathews
    B) Harry Hess and Robert Dietz   D) Alfred Wegener and Arthur Holmes
    Ans: C   Page: 36

33. Which of the following is commonly used to determine the age of seafloor samples recovered by the deep-sea drilling project?
    A) carbon-14 dating   C) foraminifera fossils
    B) chemical composition   D) gravity measurements
    Ans: C   Page: 38

34. Which of the following plates is moving the fastest?
    A) the African plate   C) the North American plate
    B) the Eurasian plate   D) the Pacific plate
    Ans: D   Page: 39

35. On a map of the seafloor, the boundaries between normally magnetized oceanic crust and reversely magnetized oceanic crust are called _____.
    A) dipoles   B) isochrons   C) isograds   D) sutures
    Ans: B   Page: 40

36. When was the supercontinent of Pangaea assembled?
    A) approximately 100 million years ago   C) approximately 1000 million years ago
    B) approximately 250 million years ago   D) approximately 2500 million years ago
    Ans: B   Page: 40

37. How old are the oldest rocks on the ocean floor?
    A) about 20 million years old   C) about 600 million years old
    B) about 200 million years old   D) about 4000 million years old
    Ans: B   Page: 41

38. The oldest continental rocks are _____ than the oldest oceanic rocks.
    A) much older   B) slightly older   C) slightly younger   D) much younger
    Ans: A   Alternative Location: Online quizzing   Page: 41

39. Isochrons on the seafloor are roughly _____ about the ridge axis along which they were created.
    A) parallel to and symmetric   C) perpendicular to and symmetric
    B) parallel to, but not symmetric,   D) perpendicular to, but not symmetric,
    Ans: A   Page: 41

40. Why are isochrons on the Pacific seafloor more widely spaced than isochrons on the Atlantic seafloor?
    A) The Pacific seafloor formed at a faster spreading rate than the Atlantic seafloor.
    B) The Pacific seafloor formed at a slower spreading rate than the Atlantic seafloor.
    C) The Pacific seafloor is older than the Atlantic seafloor.
    D) The Pacific seafloor is younger than the Atlantic seafloor.
    Ans: A   Page: 41

41. What ocean used to lie between Africa and Eurasia and was the ancestor to today's Mediterranean Sea?
    A) Gondwana   B) Panthalassa   C) Rodinia   D) Tethys
    Ans: D   Page: 43

42. When did the supercontinent Pangaea begin to break apart?
    A) about 65 million years ago   C) about 570 million years ago
    B) about 200 million years ago   D) about 1500 million years ago
    Ans: B   Page: 43

43. Pangaea split into two continents: Laurasia, made up of the northern continents, and _____, made up of the southern continents.
A) Tethys B) Panthalassa C) Gondwana D) Cascadia
Ans: C Page: 43

44. When did India begin to collide with Asia to form the Himalayas?
A) about 50 million years ago   C) about 500 million years ago
B) about 200 million years ago   D) about 2000 million years ago
Ans: A Page: 43

45. Compared to slower moving plates, faster moving plates are bounded by a greater proportion of _____.
A) continent collision zones   C) subduction zones
B) mid-ocean ridges   D) transform faults
Ans: C Alternative Location: Online quizzing Page: 44

46. What drives plate tectonics?
A) magnetic reversals B) mantle convection C) solar energy D) volcanism
Ans: B Page: 44

47. Which of the following forces is important in driving plate tectonics?
A) the pulling force of a sinking lithospheric slab
B) the pushing force of a plate sliding off a mid-ocean ridge
C) the suction force of a retreating subduction zone
D) all of the above
Ans: D Page: 45

48. How deep are plates subducted?
A) 100 km B) 700 km C) 2900 km D) 6400 km
Ans: C Page: 45

49. Regions, like Hawaii, of intense localized volcanism form above plumes of fast-rising material that originate in the _____.
A) crust B) deep mantle C) lithosphere D) outer core
Ans: B Page: 46

50. The Hawaiian volcanoes are _____.
A) located at a convergent plate boundary C) located at a transform plate boundary
B) located at a divergent plate boundary   D) not located at a plate boundary
Ans: D Page: 46

Chapter 3: Minerals: Building Blocks of Rocks

1. What is limestone made of?
   A) calcite   B) feldspar   C) olivine   D) quartz
   Ans: A   Page: 52

2. Solid materials that do not possess an orderly arrangement of atoms are called _____ .
   A) glasses   B) minerals   C) crystals   D) polymorphs
   Ans: A   Page: 52

3. Which of the following substances is not considered a mineral?
   A) coal   B) diamond   C) gypsum   D) rock salt
   Ans: A   Page: 52

4. Isotopes of a given element have _____.
   A) the same number of protons and the same atomic mass
   B) the same number of protons, but different atomic masses
   C) different numbers of protons, but the same atomic mass
   D) different numbers of protons and different atomic masses
   Ans: B   Page: 53

5. Which of the following subatomic particles has a positive charge?
   A) electron   B) neutron   C) proton   D) all of the above
   Ans: C   Page: 53

6. Sodium has an atomic number of 11. How many electrons will the sodium ion, Na^+, have?
   A) 1   B) 10   C) 11   D) 12
   Ans: B   Page: 53

7. Isotopes of an element have different numbers of _____.
   A) electrons   B) neutrons   C) protons   D) electrons, neutrons, and protons
   Ans: B   Page: 53

8. What is the name for atoms of the same element that have different numbers of neutrons?
   A) electrons   B) ions   C) isotopes   D) polymorphs
   Ans: C   Page: 53

9. Carbon has an atomic number of 6 and an atomic weight of 12.011. This means that carbon atoms have _____.
   A) 6 protons and 12.011 neutrons
   B) 6 neutrons and 12.011 protons
   C) 6 protons and a density of 12.011 grams per cubic centimeter
   D) 6 protons and varying numbers of neutrons
   Ans: D   Page: 53

10. The atomic mass of an element is equal to the number of _____.
    A) protons   C) protons plus neutrons
    B) neutrons   D) protons plus neutrons plus electrons
    Ans: C   Page: 53

11. What will be the charge of an atom containing 8 protons, 9 neutrons, and 10 electrons?
    A) –2   B) –1   C) +1   D) +2
    Ans: A   Page: 53-54

12. How are the elements organized in the periodic table?
    A) in order of increasing density
    B) in order of increasing number of electrons
    C) in order of increasing number of neutrons
    D) in order of increasing number of protons
    Ans: D   Page: 53-54

13. What does the symbol Na^+ represent?
    A) a sodium proton   C) a sodium cation
    B) a sodium electron   D) a sodium anion
    Ans: C   Page: 54

14. In order to make a sodium (Na) – chlorine (Cl) bond in NaCl, _____.
    A) one electron is transferred from the chlorine atom to the sodium atom
    B) one electron is transferred from the sodium atom to the chlorine atom
    C) two electrons are transferred from the chlorine atom to the sodium atom
    D) two electrons are transferred from the sodium atom to the chlorine atom
    Ans: B   Page: 54

15. Which of the following elements tends to share electrons?
    A) carbon   B) helium   C) oxygen   D) sodium
    Ans: A   Page: 55

16. What is the dominant type of bonding in minerals?
    A) covalent bonding   B) ionic bonding   C) metallic bonding   D) nuclear bonding
    Ans: B   Page: 56

17. Diamond is an example of what type of bonding?
    A) covalent   B) ionic   C) metallic   D) nuclear
    Ans: A   Page: 56

18. The growth of a solid from a gas or liquid whose atoms can come together in the proper chemical proportions and crystalline arrangement is called _____ .
    A) bonding   B) crystallization   C) density   D) melting
    Ans: B   Page: 56

Use the following to answer question 19:

19. What elements could be represented by the open and solid spheres in the mineral structure depicted above?
    A) carbon and oxygen
    B) iron and magnesium
    C) silicon and oxygen
    D) sodium and chlorine
    Ans: D   Page: 56

20. Which of the following statements is <u>true</u>?
    A) Cations are generally larger than anions.
    B) Cations are generally smaller than anions.
    C) Cations and anions are approximately the same size.
    D) About one-half of the cations are larger than anions and one-half are smaller.
    Ans: B   Page: 57

21. The chemical formula $(Mg,Fe)_2SiO_4$ describes which of the following minerals?
    A) feldspar   B) mica   C) olivine   D) pyroxene
    Ans: C   Page: 57

22. Iron and magnesium ions are similar in size and both have a "+2" positive charge. Therefore, we would expect iron and magnesium to _____ .
    A) bond easily
    B) form polymorphs
    C) share electrons
    D) substitute for each other in minerals
    Ans: D   Page: 57

23. Large crystals with well-formed crystal faces tend to form when _____ .
    A) minerals have space to grow   C) rocks undergo melting
    B) molten rock cools quickly   D) volcanoes erupt explosively
    Ans: A   Page: 58

24. Chemical substances that have exactly the same chemical formula but different crystal structures are called _____ .
    A) electrons   B) ions   C) isotopes   D) polymorphs
    Ans: D   Page: 58

25. Which of the following statements about graphite and diamond is <u>false</u>?
    A) Graphite and diamond have the same density.
    B) Graphite and diamond have different mineral structures.
    C) Graphite and diamond are both made of carbon atoms.
    D) Graphite is stable in the Earth's crust whereas diamond is stable in the Earth's mantle.
    Ans: A   Page: 58-60

Use the following to answer question 26:

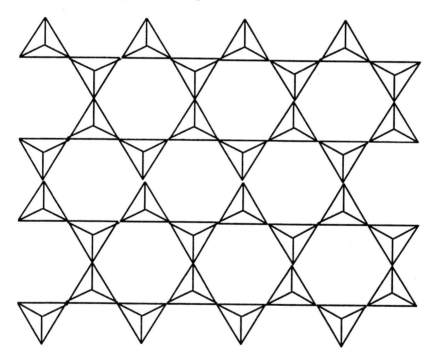

26. What silicate mineral contains tetrahedra linked together as depicted in the diagram above?
    A) amphibole   B) mica   C) pyroxene   D) quartz
    Ans: A   Page: 59

27. Which of the following structures best depicts a silicate ion?

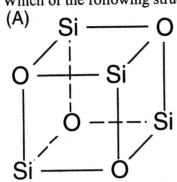

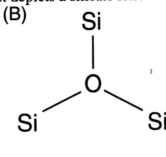

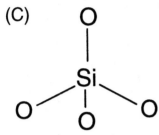

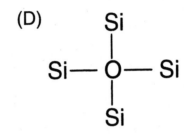

A) Diagram A   B) Diagram B   C) Diagram C   D) Diagram D
Ans: C   Page: 59

28. Most common rock-forming minerals are _____ .
A) carbonates   B) oxides   C) silicates   D) sulfides
Ans: C   Page: 60

29. The two most common elements in the Earth's crust are:
A) calcium and carbon   C) iron and sulfur
B) chlorine and sodium   D) oxygen and silicon
Ans: D   Page: 60

30. Which of the following minerals is a common clay mineral used for making pottery?
A) feldspar   B) kaolinite   C) olivine   D) pyroxene
Ans: B   Page: 61

31. Which of the following statements about feldspar is false?
A) Feldspar is harder than calcite.
B) Feldspar is softer than corundum
C) Feldspar is the most abundant mineral in the Earth's crust.
D) Feldspar is a sheet silicate.
Ans: D   Page: 61

32. What type of minerals are calcite and dolomite?
A) carbonates   B) oxides   C) silicates   D) sulfates
Ans: A   Page: 61

33. Mica is a common example of a _____ silicate.
    A) framework   B) single chain   C) double chain   D) sheet
    Ans: D   Page: 61

34. Which of the following atomic structures represents a carbonate ion?

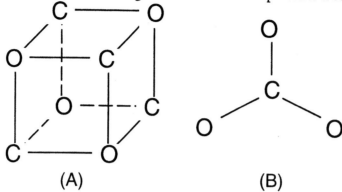

(A)   (B)

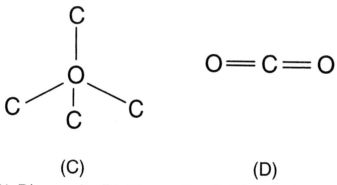

(C)   (D)

    A) Diagram A   B) Diagram B   C) Diagram C   D) Diagram D
    Ans: B   Page: 61

35. Which of the following minerals does not contain carbon?
    A) calcite   B) diamond   C) dolomite   D) gypsum
    Ans: D   Page: 62

36. What type of mineral is gypsum, the primary component of plaster?
    A) carbonate   B) oxide   C) silicate   D) sulfate
    Ans: D   Page: 62

37. What type of mineral is pyrite, also known as "fool's gold"?
    A) carbonate   B) oxide   C) silicate   D) sulfide
    Ans: D   Page: 62

38. What form of iron is the chief iron ore?
    A) iron carbonate   B) iron oxide   C) iron sulfide   D) native iron metal
    Ans: B   Page: 62

39. Which of the following metals is commonly mined as an oxide?
    A) iron   B) nickel   C) copper   D) zinc
    Ans: A   Page: 62

40. Which of the following minerals fizzes when it comes in contact with hydrochloric acid (HCl)?
    A) calcite   B) halite   C) mica   D) quartz
    Ans: A   Page: 63

41. What is the hardest mineral?
    A) calcite   B) corundum   C) diamond   D) quartz
    Ans: C   Page: 63

42. Which of the following minerals has the greatest hardness?
    A) calcite   B) orthoclase   C) quartz   D) talc
    Ans: C   Page: 63

43. Which of the following minerals is not a form of Al_2O_3?
    A) corundum   B) diamond   C) ruby   D) sapphire
    Ans: B   Page: 64

44. The mineral property "cleavage" refers to _____.
    A) the development of crystal faces during mineral growth
    B) the splitting of a mineral along planar surfaces
    C) the development of irregular fractures in a mineral
    D) the density of a mineral
    Ans: B   Page: 65

45. When cleaved, mica breaks through planes of _____.
    A) aluminum hydroxide
    B) interlayer cations
    C) silicon-oxygen tetrahedra
    D) sulfate anions
    Ans: B   Page: 65

46. Which of the following minerals has the best cleavage?
    A) amphibole   B) mica   C) pyroxene   D) quartz
    Ans: B   Page: 66

47. Which of the following minerals has two good cleavage planes oriented at right angles to each other?
    A) amphibole   B) calcite   C) mica   D) pyroxene
    Ans: D   Page: 66

48. Which of the following minerals does not exhibit cleavage?
    A) amphibole   B) calcite   C) mica   D) quartz
    Ans: D   Page: 66

49. Which of the following statements regarding the density of minerals is <u>false</u>?
    A) Density depends on the atomic weight of the ions in a mineral.
    B) Density depends on the closeness of the atomic packing.
    C) Density increases with increasing pressure.
    D) Density increases with increasing temperature.
    Ans: D   Page: 68

50. Which of the following statements about asbestos is <u>false</u>?
    A) Only one asbestos mineral, crocidolite, forms sharp fibers.
    B) Most asbestos minerals are amphiboles.
    C) U.S. government regulations apply only to the asbestos mineral crocidolite.
    D) Several fatal lung diseases have been linked to inhaling certain kinds of asbestos.
    Ans: C   Page: 69

Chapter 4: Rocks: Records of Geologic Processes

1. What two properties determine a rock's appearance?
   A) cleavage and hardness
   B) color and density
   C) fracture and luster
   D) mineralogy and texture
   Ans: D   Page: 75

2. A rock's mineralogy refers to the _____.
   A) kinds and proportions of minerals in a rock
   B) relative size of the mineral grains
   C) value of a rock if it were mined for precious metals
   D) weight percent of each element in a rock
   Ans: A   Page: 75

3. The texture of a rock is its _____.
   A) density referenced to water
   B) overall size, shape, and degree of weathering
   C) roughness and specific gravity
   D) size, shape, and spatial arrangement of mineral grains
   Ans: D   Page: 75

4. How do igneous rocks form?
   A) by biochemical precipitation of minerals
   B) by lithification of sediments
   C) by solid state changes under high temperature and pressure
   D) by solidification of molten rock
   Ans: D   Page: 75

5. How do metamorphic rocks form?
   A) by biochemical precipitation of minerals
   B) by lithification of sediments
   C) by solid state changes under high temperature and pressure
   D) by solidification of molten rock
   Ans: C   Page: 76

6. What type of rocks form from layers of sand and mud?
   A) chemical sedimentary
   B) clastic sedimentary
   C) plutonic igneous
   D) volcanic igneous
   Ans: B   Page: 76

7. In what type of rock does oil form?
   A) metamorphic rocks   C) sedimentary rocks
   B) plutonic rocks   D) volcanic rocks
   Ans: C   Page: 76

8. Which of the following rocks is not a metamorphic rock?
   A) gneiss   B) granite   C) marble   D) schist
   Ans: B   Page: 76-77

9. What type of rocks form from crystallization of a magma?
   A) igneous rocks   C) sedimentary rocks
   B) metamorphic rocks   D) all of the above
   Ans: A   Page: 77

10. The temperature needed to melt most rocks is at least _____.
    A) 100 °C   B) 250 °C   C) 700 °C   D) 1500 °C
    Ans: C   Page: 77

11. Volcanic rocks have smaller crystals than plutonic rocks because _____.
    A) plutonic rocks cool slower than volcanic rocks
    B) volcanic rocks cool slower than plutonic rocks
    C) plutonic rocks melt slower than volcanic rocks
    D) volcanic rocks melt slower than plutonic rocks
    Ans: A   Page: 77-78

12. Which of the following statements regarding igneous rocks is false?
    A) Extrusive rocks have larger crystals than intrusive rocks.
    B) Extrusive rocks cool more rapidly than intrusive rocks.
    C) Intrusive igneous rocks form deep in the crust or upper mantle.
    D) Intrusive and extrusive igneous rocks have the same range of chemical compositions.
    Ans: A   Page: 77-78

13. Which of the following statements about extrusive igneous rocks is false?
    A) Extrusive igneous rocks generally contain fine-grained crystals and/or glass.
    B) Extrusive igneous rocks may contain feldspar, pyroxene, and mica.
    C) Extrusive igneous rocks cover most of the surface of the continents.
    D) Extrusive igneous rocks cool rapidly from a magma.
    Ans: C   Page: 77

14. Which of the following scenarios will form an igneous rock with the smallest crystals?
    A) a magma extruded onto the Earth's surface
    B) a magma intruded at 10 km depth in the Earth
    C) a magma intruded at 40 km depth in the Earth
    D) All of the above will form rocks with the same crystal size.
    Ans: A   Page: 78

15. What type of rock is illustrated in the diagram below?

    ol = olivine crystals
    plag = plagioclase feldspar crystals
    px = pyroxene crystals

    A) extrusive igneous rock   C) metamorphic rock
    B) intrusive igneous rock   D) sedimentary rock
    Ans: B   Page: 77-78

16. Most of the minerals in igneous rocks are _____.
    A) carbonates   B) hydrates   C) silicates   D) sulfates
    Ans: C   Page: 77

17. Which of the following sets of minerals is not commonly found in an igneous rock?
    A) amphibole, feldspar, pyroxene   C) feldspar, mica, quartz
    B) calcite, garnet, mica   D) feldspar, olivine, pyroxene
    Ans: B   Page: 78

18. Which of the following minerals is commonly found only in metamorphic rocks?
    A) feldspar   B) kyanite   C) mica   D) quartz
    Ans: B   Page: 78

19. Which of the following rocks is best described as a clastic sedimentary rock?
    A) granite   B) rock salt   C) sandstone   D) schist
    Ans: C   Page: 78-79

20. Which of the following processes is not part of the formation of a sedimentary rock?
    A) burial   B) deposition   C) intrusion   D) lithification
    Ans: C   Page: 79

21. Chemical sediments form from _____.
    A) accumulation of calcium carbonate shells
    B) rapid cooling of molten sediments
    C) particles of sediment deposited in water
    D) precipitation of minerals from sea water
    Ans: D   Page: 78

22. What type of rock is sandstone?
    A) chemical sedimentary rock
    B) clastic sedimentary rock
    C) contact metamorphic rock
    D) regional metamorphic rock
    Ans: B   Page: 79

23. How do clastic sediments form?
    A) by crystallization of sediments from magma
    B) by deposition of sediment particles
    C) by lithification of sand particles
    D) by precipitation of sediments from sea water
    Ans: B   Page: 78-79

24. Which of the following processes involves solid-state mineral changes that occur in a rock as a result of high temperature and pressure?
    A) chemical precipitation   B) metamorphism   C) plutonism   D) volcanism
    Ans: B   Page: 80

25. At what temperature do new minerals begin to appear during metamorphism?
    A) 100 °C   B) 250 °C   C) 700 °C   D) 1500 °C
    Ans: B   Page: 80

26. What is limestone composed of?
    A) calcium carbonate   B) calcium sulfate   C) silicon dioxide   D) sodium chloride
    Ans: A   Page: 79

27. Which of the following rock types is the least abundant in the Earth's crust?
    A) igneous
    B) metamorphic
    C) sedimentary
    D) igneous, metamorphic, and sedimentary rocks are equally abundant
    Ans: C   Page: 79

28. What type of rock is halite, which forms from the precipitation of sodium chloride?
    A) chemical sedimentary rock
    B) clastic sedimentary rock
    C) extrusive igneous rock
    D) intrusive igneous rock
    Ans: A   Page: 79

29. Which rock type undergoes mineralogical and textural changes to form a metamorphic rock?
    A) igneous rocks
    B) metamorphic rocks
    C) sedimentary rocks
    D) all of the above
    Ans: D   Page: 80

30. Which of the following features is diagnostic of a sedimentary rock?
    A) bedding B) cleavage C) foliation D) glassy texture
    Ans: A   Page: 79

31. Which of the following does not form from molten rock?
    A) basalt B) granite C) limestone D) volcanic ash
    Ans: C   Page: 79

32. Which of the following statements regarding metamorphic rocks is true?
    A) Metamorphic rocks undergo partial melting that changes their mineralogy.
    B) Metamorphic rocks only form deep in the Earth's mantle where pressures and
       temperatures are high.
    C) All metamorphic rocks exhibit foliation, which is a characteristic and distinguishing
       feature.
    D) Metamorphic rocks are commonly found at convergent plate boundaries and near
       igneous intrusions.
    Ans: D   Page: 80-81

33. Which of the following rocks is best described as a foliated metamorphic rock?
    A) basalt B) granite C) sandstone D) schist
    Ans: D   Page: 80

34. A schist is an example of a _____ rock.
    A) contact metamorphic   C) regional metamorphic
    B) plutonic igneous   D) volcanic igneous
    Ans: C   Page: 80

35. Which of the following features is diagnostic of a regionally metamorphosed rock?
    A) bedding B) foliation C) glassy texture D) low density
    Ans: B   Page: 80

36. What type of metamorphism occurs where oceanic crust subducts beneath the leading
    edge of a continental plate?
    A) contact metamorphism
    B) high-pressure, low-temperature metamorphism
    C) regional metamorphism
    D) ultra-high-pressure metamorphism
    Ans: B   Page: 81

37. Which of the following rock types best records changes in pressure-temperature
    conditions over time?
    A) extrusive igneous rocks   C) metamorphic rocks
    B) intrusive igneous rocks   D) sedimentary rocks
    Ans: C   Page: 80

38. How deep has the deepest continental hole penetrated?
    A) into the upper continental crust   C) into the upper mantle
    B) into the lower continental crust   D) into the lower mantle
    Ans: A   Page: 80-81

39. Outcrops are most abundant in which of the following locations in the U.S.?
    A) Central east coast   B) Great Plains   C) Midwest   D) Pacific Coast
    Ans: D   Page: 81

40. Bedrock is _____.
    A) beds of clastic sedimentary rock
    B) rock that has not been deformed during regional metamorphism
    C) rock underlying loose surface material
    D) volcanic rock
    Ans: C   Page: 81

41. In the American Midwest outcrop is scarce because _____.
    A) bedrock is virtually non-existent.
    B) extensive building construction has not occurred.
    C) soil and sediments deposited by rivers cover the bedrock.
    D) volcanic ash covers the bedrock.
    Ans: C   Page: 82

42. The presence and type of outcrops do not depend upon the _____.
    A) age of the region's rocks   C) nature of the landscape
    B) geologic structure of the region   D) present climate of the region
    Ans: A   Page: 82-83

43. The rock cycle is a result of interaction between which two Earth systems?
    A) climate and geodynamo   C) geodynamo and plate tectonics
    B) climate and plate tectonics   D) none of the above
    Ans: B   Page: 83

44. Which of the following is not likely to occur when an igneous rock is exposed to cool, wet surroundings?
    A) Feldspars may become clay minerals.   C) Pyroxene may dissolve.
    B) Iron minerals may form iron oxides.   D) Quartz may melt.
    Ans: D   Page: 83

45. Subsidence of the Earth's crust promotes _____.
    A) accumulation of layers of sediment
    B) melting of sediments
    C) metamorphism
    D) weathering of rock near the Earth's surface
    Ans: A   Page: 85

46. The rock cycle is _____.
    A) a set of geologic processes by which rocks are formed from other rocks
    B) a period of approximately 100 million years during which all of the Earth's rocks are remade into new rocks
    C) a circuit from oceanic spreading center to subduction zone
    D) the transformation of clastic sedimentary rocks into chemical sedimentary rock
    Ans: A   Page: 83-85

47. Orogeny occurs at which type of plate boundary?
    A) convergent plate boundaries   C) transform plate boundaries
    B) divergent plate boundaries   D) all of the above
    Ans: A   Page: 83

Use the following to answer questions 48-50:

The following questions refer to the diagram below:

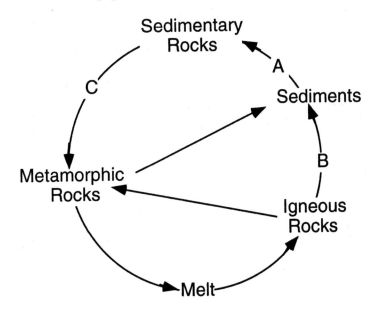

48. Referring to the diagram above, path "A" is _____?
    A) burial and lithification   C) cooling and uplift
    B) cooling and crystallization   D) weathering and deposition
    Ans: A   Page: 83-85

49. Referring to the diagram above, what must occur along path "B"?
    A) deposition, heat and pressure, weathering
    B) deposition, lithification, crystallization
    C) melting, crystallization, heat and pressure
    D) uplift, weathering and erosion, deposition
    Ans: D   Page: 83-85

50. Referring to the diagram above, what factor(s) are responsible for path "C"?
    A) burial and lithification   B) crystallization   C) heat and pressure   D) melting
    Ans: C   Page: 83-85

Chapter 5: Igneous Rocks: Solids from Melts

1. Where would you expect to find the largest crystals in a lava flow?
   A) near the top surface of the flow
   B) in the center of the flow
   C) near the bottom surface of the flow
   D) the crystals would be the same size throughout
   Ans: B   Page: 90

2. Which of the following properties does <u>not</u> depend on the chemical composition of an igneous rock/magma?
   A) grain size   B) melting temperature   C) mineralogy   D) viscosity
   Ans: A   Page: 90-91

3. What geologist is credited with figuring out the origin of granite?
   A) N.L. Bowen   B) Charles Darwin   C) James Hutton   D) Alfred Wegener
   Ans: C   Page: 90-91

4. Which of the following igneous rocks crystallizes near the Earth's surface?
   A) basalt   B) gabbro   C) granite   D) peridotite
   Ans: A   Page: 91-92

5. What type of volcanic rock contains a large number of vesicles (bubbles) that form when gases escape from the solidifying melt?
   A) granite   B) obsidian   C) porphyry   D) pumice
   Ans: D   Page: 92

6. Which of the following rocks is a volcanic rock made up of lithified pyroclastic material?
   A) basalt   B) granodiorite   C) obsidian   D) tuff
   Ans: D   Page: 91-92

7. Felsic igneous rocks contain abundant _____ silicate minerals.
   A) double-chain   B) framework   C) isolated tetrahedra   D) single-chain
   Ans: B   Page: 92-93

8. Which of the following best describes a rock with 10-millimeter-long plagioclase crystals set in a fine-grained matrix of 0.5-millimeter-long crystals?
   A) obsidian   B) pluton   C) porphyry   D) tuff
   Ans: C   Page: 92

9. Which of the following igneous rocks does <u>not</u> consist of volcanic glass?
   A) ash   B) gabbro   C) obsidian   D) pumice
   Ans: B   Page: 92

10. What is the approximate silica content of a granite?
    A) 30%   B) 50%   C) 70%   D) 90%
    Ans: C   Page: 93

11. Which of the following minerals is common in both felsic and mafic igneous rocks?
    A) olivine   B) plagioclase feldspar   C) pyroxene   D) quartz
    Ans: B   Page: 93

12. Which of the following igneous rocks has the lowest silica content?
    A) felsic   B) intermediate   C) mafic   D) ultramafic
    Ans: D   Page: 93

13. Which of the following best describes a rhyolite?
    A) fine-grained igneous rock rich in silica
    B) fine-grained igneous rock poor in silica
    C) coarse-grained igneous rock rich in silica
    D) coarse-grained igneous rock poor in silica
    Ans: A   Page: 93

14. Which of the following minerals is <u>rarely</u> found in felsic igneous rocks?
    A) olivine   B) orthoclase feldspar   C) plagioclase feldspar   D) quartz
    Ans: A   Page: 92-93

Use the following to answer question 15:

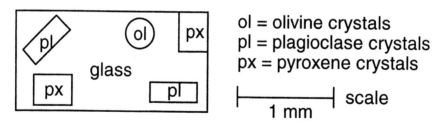

15. Which of the following best describes the igneous rock depicted in the diagram above?
    A) andesite   B) basalt   C) granite   D) peridotite
    Ans: B   Page: 93-94

Use the following to answer question 16:

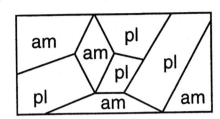 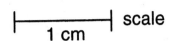

am = amphibole crystals
pl = plagioclase feldspar crystals

scale
1 cm

16. Which of the following best describes the igneous rock depicted in the diagram above?
    A) basalt   B) diorite   C) granite   D) rhyolite
    Ans: B   Page: 94

17. Andesite is an example of a(n) _____ igneous rock.
    A) felsic   B) intermediate   C) mafic   D) ultramafic
    Ans: B   Page: 94-95

18. Which of the following best describes an andesite?
    A) a coarse-grained, intermediate igneous rock
    B) a fine-grained, intermediate igneous rock
    C) a coarse-grained, felsic igneous rock
    D) a fine-grained, felsic igneous rock
    Ans: B   Page: 95

19. Which of the following types of igneous rocks are rarely found as lavas?
    A) felsic   B) intermediate   C) mafic   D) ultramafic
    Ans: D   Page: 94

20. Which of the following igneous rocks has the same chemical composition as basalt?
    A) andesite   B) diorite   C) gabbro   D) rhyolite
    Ans: C   Page: 95

21. Which of the following pairs of intrusive and extrusive rocks have the same chemical
    composition?
    A) diorite and rhyolite   C) gabbro and rhyolite
    B) gabbro and basalt   D) granite and andesite
    Ans: B   Page: 95

22. Which igneous rock is the most abundant igneous rock of the crust and underlies
    virtually all of the floors of the ocean?
    A) andesite   B) basalt   C) granite   D) peridotite
    Ans: B   Page: 94

23. Which of the following properties <u>increases</u> in the direction of the arrows in the diagram below?

Felsic ⟶ Intermediate ⟶ Mafic

   A) melting temperature   B) potassium content   C) silica content   D) viscosity
   Ans: A   Page: 95

24. Which of the following statements is <u>true</u>?
   A) Gabbro has a higher melting temperature than granite.
   B) Gabbro has a higher potassium content than granite.
   C) Gabbro has a higher silica content than granite.
   D) Gabbro has a higher viscosity than granite.
   Ans: A   Page: 95

25. Which of the following statements about felsic igneous rocks is <u>true</u>?
   A) Felsic rocks contain less silica than mafic rocks.
   B) Felsic rocks crystallize at lower temperatures than mafic rocks.
   C) Felsic rocks tend to be darker-colored than mafic rocks.
   D) Felsic rocks tend to be finer-grained than mafic rocks.
   Ans: B   Page: 95

26. Which of the following types of igneous rocks crystallizes deep within the Earth's crust?
   A) andesite   B) basalt   C) gabbro   D) rhyolite
   Ans: C   Page: 95

27. Which of the following lists is in the correct order of <u>increasing</u> silica content?
   A) diorite → granite → gabbro   C) gabbro → diorite → granite
   B) gabbro → granite → diorite   D) granite → diorite → gabbro
   Ans: C   Page: 95

28. For a rock of a specific composition, which of the following statements is <u>true</u>?
   A) The amount of partial melt decreases with increasing temperature.
   B) The melting temperature increases with increasing pressure.
   C) The melting temperature increases with increasing water content.
   D) <u>All</u> of the above are true.
   Ans: B   Page: 95

29. How fast do magmas rise through the crust?
   A) a few microns per year   C) a few meters per year
   B) a few millimeters per year   D) a few kilometers per year
   Ans: C   Page: 97

30. What composition is the Palisades sill located near New York?
   A) felsic   B) intermediate   C) mafic   D) ultramafic
   Ans: C   Page: 98-99

31. At approximately what temperature do olivine and calcium-rich plagioclase feldspar crystallize from a magma?
    A) 300 °C   B) 600 °C   C) 1200 °C   D) 2000 °C
    Ans: C   Page: 98-99

32. Which of the following minerals is most likely to settle to the bottom of a magma chamber?
    A) olivine   B) plagioclase feldspar   C) pyroxene   D) quartz
    Ans: A   Page: 98-99

33. Which of the following minerals crystallizes from a magma at the lowest temperature?
    A) calcium-rich feldspar   B) olivine   C) pyroxene   D) quartz
    Ans: D   Page: 98

34. Which of the following processes would most likely yield a granitic magma?
    A) partial melting of subducted oceanic crust and sediments
    B) partial melting of the continental crust
    C) partial melting of the core
    D) partial melting of the upper mantle
    Ans: B   Page: 99-100

35. Large igneous bodies that form at depth in the Earth's crust are called _____.
    A) dikes   B) plutons   C) sills   D) veins
    Ans: B   Page: 101

Use the following to answer question 36:

36. Which of the following best describes the gray igneous rock depicted in the cross section above?
    A) dike   B) lava flow   C) pluton   D) sill
    Ans: A   Page: 101-102

37. In order to rise through the crust, magmas make space by all of the following processes except _____.
    A) by breaking off large blocks of rock that sink into the magma chamber
    B) by following preexisting networks of caverns
    C) by melting surrounding rocks
    D) by wedging open the overlying rock
    Ans: B   Page: 101

38. Which of the following igneous bodies is a concordant intrusive rock?
    A) dike   B) pluton   C) sill   D) stock
    Ans: C   Page: 101-102

39. How can a sill be distinguished from a lava flow?
    A) A sill is generally finer-grained than a lava flow.
    B) Rocks above and below a sill will show evidence of heating, but only the rocks below a lava flow will show evidence of heating.
    C) Sills generally have vesicles; lava flows generally do not have vesicles.
    D) Sills generally overlie soils; lava flows do not generally overlie soils.
    Ans: B   Page: 102

40. The famous Mother Lode of the 1849 California gold rush is an example of

    _____.
    A) a basaltic dike   B) a volcanic tuff   C) a hydrothermal vein   D) a granitic pluton
    Ans: C   Page: 102

41. Which of the following are mined for rare elements, such as lithium and beryllium?
    A) dacites   B) gabbros   C) pegmatites   D) tuffs
    Ans: C   Page: 102

42. At what temperature do minerals crystallize in hydrothermal veins?
    A) approximately 300 °C   C) approximately 900 °C
    B) approximately 600 °C   D) approximately 1500 °C
    Ans: A   Page: 103

43. What type of rock makes up most of the Hawaiian Islands?
    A) andesite   B) basalt   C) granite   D) peridotite
    Ans: B   Page: 104

44. Which of the following is not part of an ophiolite suite?
    A) basaltic dikes   C) granitic plutons
    B) deep-sea sediments   D) massive gabbros
    Ans: C   Page: 105

45. What type of magma forms at mid-ocean ridges?
    A) felsic   B) intermediate   C) mafic   D) ultramafic
    Ans: C   Page: 104-105

46. What type of magma forms when mantle undergoes decompression melting?
    A) felsic   B) intermediate   C) mafic   D) ultramafic
    Ans: C   Page: 104-105

47. Which of the following magma compositions will be produced by partial melting of the upper mantle?
    A) felsic   B) intermediate   C) mafic   D) ultramafic
    Ans: C   Page: 106-107

48. Compared to the mantle beneath a mid-ocean ridge, the mantle above a subduction zone _____.
    A) contains less water and melts at a lower temperature
    B) contains less water and melts at a higher temperature
    C) contains more water and melts at a lower temperature
    D) contains more water and melts at a higher temperature
    Ans: C   Page: 107-108

49. Fluid-induced melting generates magmas in which of the following tectonic settings?
    A) mantle plumes   B) mid-ocean ridges   C) subduction zones   D) transform faults
    Ans: C   Page: 107-108

50. Which of the following tectonic settings has the greatest range in magma compositions?
    A) convergent plate boundaries   C) transform plate boundaries
    B) divergent plate boundaries   D) hot spots (mantle plumes)
    Ans: A   Page: 107-108

Chapter 6: Volcanism

1. What volcano represents a major hazard to the cities of Seattle and Tacoma in Washington state?
   A) Mt. Ranier   B) Mt. St. Helens   C) Mt. Shasta   D) Yellowstone
   Ans: A   Page: 112, 134

2. What is molten rock beneath the Earth's surface called?
   A) granite   B) lava   C) lithosphere   D) magma
   Ans: D   Page: 114

3. Where do most basaltic magmas originate?
   A) in the Earth's asthenosphere   C) in the Earth's crust
   B) in the Earth's core   D) in the Earth's lithosphere
   Ans: A   Page: 114

4. Which of the following statements about lava is <u>true</u>?
   A) The viscosity of a lava increases as the silica content decreases.
   B) High temperature lavas are less viscous than low temperature lavas.
   C) The more gas a lava contains, the less violent the eruption.
   D) <u>All</u> of the statements above are true.
   Ans: B   Page: 115

5. What is the name for a basaltic lava flow that has a ropy, folded surface?
   A) aa   B) breccia   C) pahoehoe   D) tuff
   Ans: C   Page: 115

6. What is the eruption temperature of basaltic lava?
   A) 400-600 °C   B) 600-800 °C   C) 800-1000 °C   D) 1000-1200 °C
   Ans: D   Page: 115

7. What type of rock makes up the Columbia Plateau of Oregon and Washington?
   A) cinder cones   B) composite volcanoes   C) flood basalts   D) pyroclastic flows
   Ans: C   Page: 115

Use the following to answer question 8:

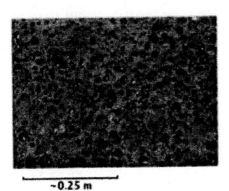

~0.25 m

8. In the basalt sample depicted above, the vesicles (small spherical cavities) most likely formed by _____.
   A) the escape of gas bubbles dissolved in the lava during the eruption
   B) the weathering and erosion of olivine crystals after the eruption
   C) air bubbles entrained in the flow during the eruption
   D) vaporization of sea water during underwater eruption
   Ans: A   Page: 116

9. Which of the following lavas will flow downhill slowest?
   A) andesite
   B) basalt
   C) rhyolite
   D) andesite, basalt, and rhyolite lavas all flow at approximately the same speed
   Ans: C   Page: 116

10. Which of the following rocks is formed from volcanic ash?
    A) aa   B) breccia   C) pahoehoe   D) tuff
    Ans: D   Page: 117

11. Solidified fragments of volcanic material ejected into the air are called _____.
    A) phenocrysts   B) pillow basalts   C) pyroclasts   D) vesicles
    Ans: C   Page: 117

12. Which of the following volcanic flows moves the most rapidly?
    A) basaltic lava flows   B) lahars   C) pyroclastic flows   D) rhyolitic lava flows
    Ans: C   Page: 118

13. Which of the following volcanic deposits is most likely to form from a felsic lava?
    A) flood basalt   B) pahoehoe   C) shield volcano   D) volcanic dome
    Ans: C   Page: 120

14. What determines the slope of a cinder cone?
    A) the extent of regional faulting
    B) the maximum angle at which cinders remain stable
    C) the maximum slope of the underlying bedrock topography
    D) the viscosity of the lava
    Ans: B   Page: 120

Use the following to answer question 15:

15. What type of volcanic flows likely formed the volcano depicted in cross section above?
    A) andesite flows   B) basalt flows   C) rhyolite flows   D) volcanic mudflows
    Ans: B   Page: 120

16. What type of volcano consists of both lava flows and pyroclastic deposits?
    A) cinder cone   B) shield volcano   C) stratovolcano   D) volcanic dome
    Ans: C   Page: 120

17. What type of volcano has the largest and most violent eruptions?
    A) cinder cones   B) fissure eruptions   C) resurgent calderas   D) shield volcanoes
    Ans: C   Page: 120

18. Which of the following volcanoes is a composite volcano (stratovolcano)?
    A) Mauna Loa, Hawaii   C) Shiprock, New Mexico
    B) Mt. Rainier, Washington   D) Yellowstone, Wyoming
    Ans: B   Page: 120

19. Yellowstone, in Wyoming, is an example of a _____.
    A) caldera   B) cinder cone   C) composite volcano   D) shield volcano
    Ans: A   Page: 120

20. How much pyroclastic debris was erupted from Yellowstone caldera 600,000 years ago?
    A) about 1 cubic kilometer   C) about 100 cubic kilometers
    B) about 10 cubic kilometers   D) about 1000 cubic kilometers
    Ans: D   Page: 120

21. The eruption of vast quantities of superheated steam is called a _____.
    A) fissure eruption   B) lava flow   C) phreatic explosion   D) resurgent caldera
    Ans: C   Page: 120

22. What type of volcanic deposit may contain diamonds such as the diamond mines of Kimberly, South Africa?
    A) cinder cones   B) diatremes   C) pahoehoe flows   D) pillow lavas
    Ans: B   Page: 120-121

23. Shiprock, New Mexico, is an example of a _____.
    A) caldera   B) cinder cone   C) diatreme   D) lava flow
    Ans: C   Page: 121-122

24. Huge mudflows made up of wet volcanic debris are called _____ .
    A) calderas   B) diatremes   C) lahars   D) tuffs
    Ans: C   Page: 123

25. Almost all of the 25,000 people killed in the 1985 eruption of Nevada del Ruiz in Columbia were killed by _____.
    A) a very thick volcanic ash fall   C) a large mudflow of volcanic debris
    B) a fast-moving lava flow   D) collapse of a volcanic caldera
    Ans: C   Page: 123

26. Which of the following statements about the May 18, 1980 climactic eruption of Mt. St. Helens is <u>false</u>?
    A) Earthquakes began to occur underneath the volcano six years before the eruption.
    B) Volcanic ash was erupted up to 25 kilometers into the atmosphere.
    C) Approximately 60 people were killed by the eruption.
    D) The eruption was immediately preceded by a large earthquake and landslide.
    Ans: A   Page: 126-127

27. Which of the following gases is the main constituent of volcanic gas?
    A) carbon dioxide   B) nitrogen   C) sulfur dioxide   D) water vapor
    Ans: D   Page: 124

28. What type of volcanic gases form aerosols in the upper atmosphere that can cause global cooling?
    A) carbon dioxide   B) nitrogen   C) sulfur dioxide   D) water vapor
    Ans: C   Page: 124

29. Which of the following volcanic gases emitted during the 1992 eruption of Mount Pinatubo increased the rate of ozone loss in the atmosphere?
    A) carbon dioxide   B) chlorine   C) sulfur dioxide   D) water vapor
    Ans: B   Page: 124

30. Small vents on volcanoes that emit gas fumes and steam are called _____.
    A) calderas   B) fumaroles   C) lahars   D) vesicles
    Ans: B   Page: 125

31. Most of the world's active volcanoes are located around the edge of which ocean?
    A) Arctic Ocean   B) Atlantic Ocean   C) Indian Ocean   D) Pacific Ocean
    Ans: D   Page: 128

32. What percentage of Earth's active volcanoes occur at divergent plate boundaries?
    A) approximately 15%   C) approximately 80%
    B) approximately 50%   D) approximately 95%
    Ans: A   Page: 128

33. In which of the following tectonic settings do most of the Earth's active volcanoes occur?
    A) convergent plate boundaries   C) transform plate boundaries
    B) divergent plate boundaries   D) intraplate settings
    Ans: A   Page: 128

34. What types of lavas are erupted at mid-ocean ridges?
    A) andesites   B) basalts   C) rhyolites   D) all of the above
    Ans: B   Page: 128

Use the following to answer questions 35-37:

The following questions refer to the plate tectonic diagram below:

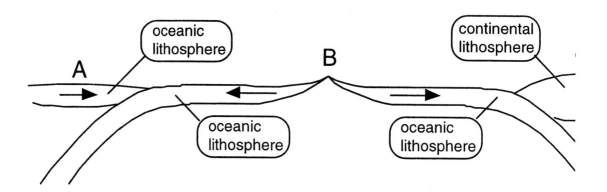

35. What type of lava is most likely to erupt at tectonic setting "B"?
    A) andesite   B) basalt   C) rhyolite   D) All of the above are equally likely.
    Ans: B   Page: 129

36. Which of the following volcanic chains formed at a tectonic setting similar to "C"?
    A) Aleutian Islands   B) Andes Mountains   C) Hawaiian Islands   D) Mariana Arc
    Ans: B   Page: 129

37. Which of the following volcanic chains formed at a tectonic setting similar to "A"?
    A) Aleutian Islands
    B) Andes Mountains
    C) Cascade Range
    D) Hawaiian Islands
    Ans: A   Page: 129

38. Approximately how much basaltic lava is erupted each year at mid-ocean ridges?
    A) 3 cubic kilometers
    B) 30 cubic kilometers
    C) 300 cubic kilometers
    D) 3000 cubic kilometers
    Ans: A   Page: 128

39. How hot are so-called "black smokers," hydrothermal vents present on the mid-ocean ridge crests?
    A) 150 °C   B) 350 °C   C) 750 °C   D) 1500 °C
    Ans: B   Page: 129

40. Metal-rich minerals precipitate out of hydrothermal vents at mid-ocean ridge crests. These minerals form ores of all of the following metals except _____.
    A) copper   B) gold   C) iron   D) zinc
    Ans: B   Page: 129

41. What types of lavas are erupted at convergent plate boundaries?
    A) andesites   B) basalts   C) rhyolites   D) all of the above
    Ans: D   Page: 130

42. The Cascade volcanoes are associated with a _____.
    A) convergent plate margin
    B) divergent plate margin
    C) transform plate margin
    D) hot spot
    Ans: A   Page: 130

43. Where are aseismic ridges located?
    A) convergent plate boundaries
    B) divergent plate boundaries
    C) transform plate boundaries
    D) intraplate regions
    Ans: D   Page: 130

44. Volcanic rocks derived from the Yellowstone hot spot get progressively older to the southwest. Based on this information, in which direction is the North American plate moving?
    A) northeast   B) northwest   C) southeast   D) southwest
    Ans: D   Page: 131

45. How fast is the North American plate moving?
    A) 25 mm/yr   B) 75 mm/yr   C) 200 mm/yr   D) 500 mm/yr
    Ans: A   Page: 131

46. One hypothesis proposes that large igneous provinces form at hot spots by mantle plumes that originate at what boundary within the Earth?
    A) crust–mantle boundary   C) mantle–outer core boundary
    B) lithosphere–asthenosphere boundary   D) outer core–inner core boundary
    Ans: C   Page: 132-133

47. Approximately how many active volcanoes are there on Earth?
    A) 50   B) 500   C) 5000   D) 50,000
    Ans: B   Page: 134

48. Which of the following is least likely to signal an impending volcanic eruption?
    A) earthquakes   B) gas emissions   C) tsunamis   D) swelling of the volcano
    Ans: C   Page: 135

49. Over the past 2000 years, which of the following volcanic hazards has caused the most fatalities?
    A) ash falls   B) lava flows   C) mud flows   D) pyroclastic flows
    Ans: D   Page: 135

50. Which of the following states has the most active volcanoes?
    A) Alaska   B) Florida   C) New York   D) Texas
    Ans: A   Page: 136

Chapter 7: Weathering and Erosion

1. What is the general process by which rocks are broken down at the Earth's surface?
   A) deposition   B) erosion   C) lithification   D) weathering
   Ans: D   Page: 141

2. In which of the following climates will chemical weathering be the most rapid?
   A) cold and dry   B) cold and humid   C) hot and dry   D) hot and humid
   Ans: D   Page: 142-143

3. Which of the following minerals is <u>most</u> stable at the Earth's surface?
   A) hematite   B) mica   C) olivine   D) pyroxene
   Ans: A   Page: 142-143

4. Which of the following minerals is <u>least</u> stable at the Earth's surface?
   A) hematite   B) olivine   C) pyroxene   D) quartz
   Ans: B   Page: 142-143

   Use the following to answer question 5:

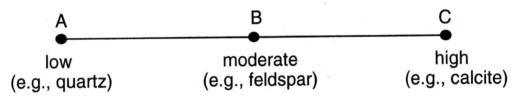

MINERAL SOLUBILITY

A
low
(e.g., quartz)

B
moderate
(e.g., feldspar)

C
high
(e.g., calcite)

5. In the figure above, where would the mineral halite plot?
   A) at point A   B) at point B   C) between points A and B   D) at point C
   Ans: D   Page: 142

Use the following to answer questions 6-7:

The following questions refer to the diagram below, which depicts relative weathering rates of different minerals.

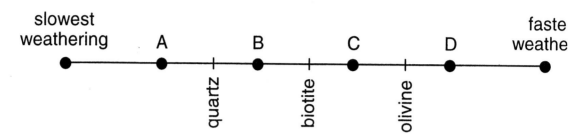

6. Where would hematite (iron oxide) plot on the diagram?
   A) point A   B) point B   C) point C   D) point D
   Ans: A   Page: 142

7. Where would calcite plot on the diagram?
   A) point A   B) point B   C) point C   D) point D
   Ans: D   Page: 142

8. Which of the following rock types will weather <u>slowest</u> in a moderately rainy climate?
   A) granite   B) halite   C) limestone   D) shale
   Ans: A   Page: 142-143

9. Which of the following promotes chemical weathering?
   A) high altitude   B) low temperature   C) sparse vegetation   D) thick soil
   Ans: D   Page: 143

10. Which of the following statements about weathering is <u>false</u>?
    A) Rocks of different compositions weather at different rates.
    B) Heat and heavy rainfall increase the rate of chemical weathering.
    C) The presence of soil slows down weathering of the underlying bedrock.
    D) The longer a rock is exposed at the surface, the more weathered it becomes.
    Ans: C   Page: 143-144

11. Which of the following statements is <u>false</u>?
    A) Soil protects the underlying bedrock from further chemical weathering.
    B) Soil is an important natural resource.
    C) Soil may contain fragments of bedrock, clay minerals, and organic matter.
    D) Soil is a product of weathering.
    Ans: A   Page: 144-145

12. A mineral that undergoes hydration _____.
    A) changes iron from ferric to ferrous   C) gains water
    B) dissolves   D) weathers into a more stable phase
    Ans: C   Page: 145

13. Which of the following minerals, present in a granite, is <u>not</u> altered by chemical weathering?
    A) biotite   B) feldspar   C) magnetite   D) quartz
    Ans: D   Page: 144

14. Which of the following minerals is <u>most</u> likely to form a clay mineral during weathering?
    A) calcite   B) feldspar   C) iron pyroxene   D) quartz
    Ans: B   Page: 144

Use the following to answer question 15:

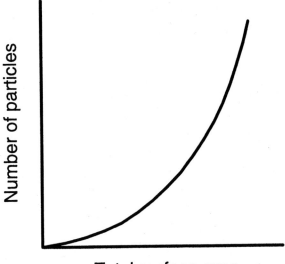

15. The diagram above depicts how the total surface area of a rock varies with the number of particles <u>for a fixed volume of rock</u>. Based on this diagram, what can be said about the ratio of surface area to volume?
    A) The ratio decreases as the number of particles increases.
    B) The ratio increases as the number of particles increases.
    C) The ratio first decreases then increases as the number of particles increases.
    D) The ratio does <u>not</u> depend on the number of particles.
    Ans: B   Page: 145-146

16. As a rock breaks into smaller pieces, the ratio of surface area to volume _____.
    A) decreases
    B) increases
    C) remains the same
    D) can either increase or decrease depending on the size of the pieces
    Ans: B   Alternative Location: Online quizzing   Page: 145-146

17. Which of the following chemical species is not produced by the chemical weathering of potassium feldspar (orthoclase)?
    A) $Al_2Si_2O_5(OH)_4$ (kaolinite, a clay mineral)
    B) H_2O (water)
    C) K^+ (potassium ion)
    D) SiO_2 (dissolved silica)
    Ans: B   Page: 146-148

18. Acids enhance chemical weathering. What is the most common natural acid on the Earth's surface?
    A) carbonic acid   B) hydrochloric acid   C) nitric acid   D) sulfuric acid
    Ans: A   Page: 146

19. What of the following acids is not an abundant acid in acid rain?
    A) carbonic acid   B) hydrochloric acid   C) nitric acid   D) sulfuric acid
    Ans: B   Page: 146-148

20. In the atmosphere, carbonic acid forms from the reaction of carbon dioxide and _____.
    A) fossil fuels   B) nitrogen   C) oxygen   D) water
    Ans: D   Page: 147

21. What happens to the potassium (K) in feldspar during chemical weathering?
    A) It dissolves in the water.
    B) It becomes part of the clay mineral.
    C) It evaporates.
    D) It becomes concentrated in potassium metal deposits.
    Ans: A   Page: 147-148

22. Which of the following statements is true?
    A) Silicate weathering and volcanism both increase the amount of carbon dioxide in the atmosphere.
    B) Silicate weathering increases and volcanism decreases the amount of carbon dioxide in the atmosphere.
    C) Silicate weathering decreases and volcanism increases the amount of carbon dioxide in the atmosphere.
    D) Silicate weathering and volcanism both decrease the amount of carbon dioxide in the atmosphere.
    Ans: C   Page: 146-147

23. Which of the following statements regarding carbon dioxide is true?
    A) As carbon dioxide in the atmosphere increases, chemical weathering decreases.
    B) An increase in carbon dioxide in the atmosphere cools the climate.
    C) Chemical weathering of feldspar is not related to atmospheric carbon dioxide.
    D) Chemical weathering reduces the amount of carbon dioxide in the atmosphere.
    Ans: D   Page: 147

24. Caves are most common in which of the following rock types?
    A) basalt   B) granite   C) limestone   D) sandstone
    Ans: C   Page: 148-149

25. Which of the following factors would increase the chemical weathering rate?
    A) decreasing organic activity
    B) decreasing temperature
    C) increasing rainfall
    D) All of the above would increase the chemical weathering rate.
    Ans: C   Page: 149

26. Which of the following is a form of chemical weathering?
    A) dissolution   B) exfoliation   C) frost wedging   D) all of the above
    Ans: A   Page: 149

27. Which of the following minerals will have the greatest chemical stability?
    A) a mineral with high solubility and a high rate of dissolution
    B) a mineral with high solubility and a low rate of dissolution
    C) a mineral with low solubility and a high rate of dissolution
    D) a mineral with low solubility and a low rate of dissolution
    Ans: D   Page: 149

28. Which of the following will decrease the rate of chemical weathering of a rock at the Earth's surface?
    A) increasing the amount of acid in the rainwater
    B) decreasing the temperature
    C) breaking the rock into smaller pieces
    D) increasing the amount of surrounding soil
    Ans: B   Page: 149

29. What is solubility?
    A) Solubility is the process by which minerals precipitate from seawater
    B) Solubility is the extent to which a mineral will dissolve in water.
    C) Solubility is the absorption of water by a mineral.
    D) Solubility is a measure of the acidity of a given amount of water.
    Ans: B   Page: 149

30. What is the difference between ferrous iron and ferric iron?
    A) Ferrous iron contains fewer electrons than ferric iron.
    B) Ferrous iron contains more electrons than ferric iron.
    C) Ferrous iron contains fewer neutrons than ferric iron.
    D) Ferrous iron contains more neutrons than ferric iron.
    Ans: B   Page: 150

31. Which of the following is a clay-rich aluminum ore composed of aluminum hydroxide?
    A) bauxite   B) hematite   C) kaolinite   D) montmorillonite
    Ans: A   Page: 150

32. The symbol, Fe^{2+}, refers to _____.
    A) ferric iron   B) ferrous iron   C) hematite   D) iron metal
    Ans: B   Page: 150

33. Which of the following minerals is most susceptible to oxidation?
    A) calcite   B) feldspar   C) olivine   D) quartz
    Ans: C   Page: 150

34. What is the most abundant form of iron at the Earth's surface?
    A) bauxite   B) hematite   C) iron metal   D) magnetite
    Ans: B   Page: 150

35. _____ is a chemical reaction in which an atom or ion loses electrons.
    A) Carbonation   B) Exfoliation   C) Hydration   D) Oxidation
    Ans: D   Page: 150

36. What causes the deep red color of soils found in Georgia and other warm, humid regions?
    A) clay minerals   B) feldspar   C) iron oxides   D) quartz
    Ans: C   Page: 151

37. Which of the following processes is not an example of chemical weathering?
    A) dissolution of calcite
    B) breakdown of feldspar to form kaolinite
    C) splitting of a rock along a fracture
    D) rusting of a nail
    Ans: C   Page: 149

38. Which of the following is an example of physical weathering?
    A) the dissolution of a rock by rainwater   C) the oxidation of iron silicates in a basalt
    B) the splitting of a rock by a tree root   D) the reaction of feldspar to kaolinite
    Ans: B   Page: 152

39. Which of the following statements is true?
    A) High temperature promotes physical weathering.
    B) Frost wedging is a form of chemical weathering.
    C) Chemical weathering is promoted by gentle slopes.
    D) Clay minerals are produced primarily by physical weathering.
    Ans: C   Page: 154

40. Organic matter in the Earth's topsoil is called _____.
    A) humus   B) leaf litter   C) pedalfer   D) regolith
    Ans: A   Page: 155

41. Which soil horizon consists primarily of slightly altered, weathered bedrock?
    A) the A-horizon   B) the B-horizon   C) the C-horizon   D) none of the above
    Ans: C   Page: 155

42. In a soil profile, organic matter is found _____.
    A) primarily in the A-horizon
    B) primarily in the B-horizon
    C) primarily in the C-horizon
    D) in the A-, B-, and C-horizons in approximately equal amounts
    Ans: A   Page: 155

43. What determines the characteristics of a soil?
    A) climate
    B) type of bedrock
    C) length of time the soil has had to develop
    D) all of the above
    Ans: D   Page: 155

44. What type of soils form in moderate climates and contain insoluble minerals such as quartz, clay minerals, and iron alteration products?
    A) laterites   B) paleosols   C) pedalfers   D) pedocals
    Ans: C   Page: 155

45. Which of the following soil types is the most fertile?
    A) evaporites   B) laterites   C) pedalfers   D) pedocals
    Ans: C   Page: 155-157

46. What is a laterite?
    A) deep-red soil in which feldspar and other silicates have been completely altered
    B) good agricultural soil containing abundant insoluble minerals such as quartz and clay minerals
    C) soil rich in calcium from calcium carbonate, and low in organic matter
    D) ancient soil, sometimes over one billion years old, preserved as rock in the geological record
    Ans: A   Page: 158

47. Which of the following farming practices helps prevent the erosion of topsoil?
    A) plowing a field perpendicular to contour lines
    B) plowing a field parallel to contour lines
    C) plowing a field in the direction that water drains
    D) All of the above will help prevent the erosion of top soil.
    Ans: B   Page: 157

48. What type of soil forms in a hot, dry climate like the southwestern Unites States?
    A) laterites
    B) pedalfers
    C) pedocals
    D) All of the above may form depending on the bedrock.
    Ans: C   Page: 158

49. Which of the following is not the product of granite weathering?
    A) clay minerals
    B) ions dissolved in rainwater and soil water
    C) iron oxides
    D) olivine
    Ans: D   Page: 158-159

50. Which of the following soils is rich in calcium?
    A) evaporites   B) laterites   C) pedalfers   D) pedocals
    Ans: D   Page: 158

Chapter 8: Sediments and Sedimentary Rocks

1. Which of the following sets of processes is written in order of increasing temperature?
   A) sedimentation, metamorphism, diagenesis
   B) diagenesis, sedimentation, metamorphism
   C) sedimentation, diagenesis, metamorphism
   D) metamorphism, diagenesis, sedimentation
   Ans: C   Page: 163

2. Which of the following terms describes the alteration of sediments to sedimentary rocks after deposition?
   A) diagenesis   B) crystallization   C) precipitation   D) metamorphism
   Ans: A   Page: 164-165

3. What type of sediments are accumulations of solid fragments produced by weathering?
   A) biochemical sediments   C) clastic sediments
   B) chemical sediments   D) all of the above
   Ans: C   Page: 165

4. Which of the following minerals would be most concentrated at a site containing heavily weathered sediments?
   A) amphibole   B) feldspar   C) mica   D) quartz
   Ans: D   Page: 165

5. How fast are moderate-strength river currents that carry and deposit sand?
   A) 2 to 5 cm/s   B) 5 to 20 cm/s   C) 20 to 50 cm/s   D) 50 to 200 cm/s
   Ans: C   Page: 167

6. Which of the following statements about transportation of sediment is false?
   A) Smaller particles settle faster than larger particles.
   B) As a current slows, the largest particles start to settle.
   C) Faster currents carry larger particles than slower currents.
   D) Rivers and ocean currents move much more material than do air currents.
   Ans: A   Page: 166

7. The tendency for variations in current velocity to segregate sediments on the basis of particle size is called _____.
   A) compaction   B) lithification   C) metamorphism   D) sorting
   Ans: D   Page: 167

8. The salinity of the ocean _____.
   A) increases by approximately 1% each year
   B) remains approximately constant
   C) decreases by approximately 1% each year
   D) fluctuates by up to 10% depending on the annual rainfall
   Ans: B   Page: 168

9. Which of the following environments is an example of a shoreline environment?
   A) alluvial   B) continental shelf   C) deltaic   D) organic reef
   Ans: C   Page: 169-170

10. In which of the following sedimentary environments would gravel most likely be deposited?
    A) alluvial   B) continental shelf   C) deep sea   D) deltaic
    Ans: A   Page: 169-170

11. In which of the following environments would gravel be least likely to be deposited?
    A) alluvial   B) beach   C) deep sea   D) glacial
    Ans: C   Page: 169-170

12. Which of the following sedimentary environments is dominated by river currents and waves?
    A) alluvial   B) deep sea   C) deltaic   D) desert
    Ans: C   Page: 169-170

13. In which of the following environments are siliceous sediments deposited?
    A) deep-sea environments   C) reef environments
    B) evaporite environments   D) swamp environments
    Ans: A   Page: 171

Use the following to answer questions 14-15:

The following questions refer to the cross section of a sand dune depicted below:

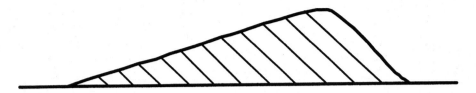

14. Assuming the sand dune was deposited by wind currents, which way was the wind blowing?
    A) ◄————————
    B) ————————►
    C) ◄————————►
    D) can't determine from the information given.
    Ans: B   Page: 172

15. The diagonal layers are called _____.
    A) cross beds   B) graded beds   C) point bars   D) ripples
    Ans: A   Page: 172

16. Which of the following is not a sedimentary structure?
    A) bioturbation   B) cross-bedding   C) foliation   D) ripples
    Ans: C   Page: 171-173

17. What is the term for the process by which organisms burrow through muds and disrupt the sedimentary bedding?
    A) biochemical precipitation   B) bioturbation   C) cementation   D) cross-bedding
    Ans: B   Page: 173

Use the following to answer question 18:

18. In what type of environment did the ripples depicted above most likely form?
    A) beach (waves)   B) desert (wind)   C) alluvial (stream)   D) delta (river + tides)
    Ans: A   Page: 172-173

19. What is the approximate temperature of a sediment that is buried to a depth of 3 km?
    A) 0 °C   B) 100 °C   C) 300 °C   D) 1000 °C
    Ans: B   Page: 174

20. Which of the following processes occurs during lithification?
    A) recrystallization of unstable minerals
    B) compaction
    C) cementation
    D) <u>All</u> of these may occur during lithification.
    Ans: D   Page: 174-175

21. Burial of sediments results in _____.
    A) decreasing pressure and decreasing temperature
    B) decreasing pressure and increasing temperature
    C) increasing pressure and decreasing temperature
    D) increasing pressure and increasing temperature
    Ans: D   Page: 174

22. What is the porosity of newly deposited mud?
    A) less than 5%   C) between 20% and 50%
    B) between 5% and 20%   D) greater than 50%
    Ans: D   Page: 175

23. Which of the following statements is <u>true</u>?
    A) Cementation and compaction both decrease porosity.
    B) Cementation increases porosity, whereas compaction decreases porosity.
    C) Cementation decreases porosity, whereas compaction increases porosity.
    D) Cementation and compaction both increase porosity.
    Ans: A   Page: 174-175

24. Which of the following lists is written in order of <u>decreasing</u> particle size?
    A) conglomerate, sandstone, siltstone   C) sandstone, siltstone, conglomerate
    B) sandstone, conglomerate, siltstone   D) siltstone, sandstone, conglomerate
    Ans: A   Page: 176

25. Which of the following is an example of a clastic sedimentary rock?
    A) chert   B) dolostone   C) evaporite   D) shale
    Ans: D   Page: 176

26. Which of the following rocks is composed of clay-sized clastic sediment?
    A) conglomerate   B) dolostone   C) sandstone   D) shale
    Ans: D   Page: 176

27. Which of the following fine-grained sedimentary rocks is clastic and displays blocky fracture and little or no bedding?
    A) chert   B) coal   C) mudstone   D) shale
    Ans: C   Page: 176

28. A clastic sedimentary rock composed of medium-grained (1 mm across) particles is called a _____.
    A) conglomerate   B) sandstone   C) shale   D) siltstone
    Ans: B   Page: 176

29. Which of the following sedimentary rock groups are <u>most</u> abundant?
    A) cherts and evaporites   C) sandstones and conglomerates
    B) limestones and dolostones   D) siltstones, mudstones, and shales
    Ans: D   Alternative Location: Online quizzing   Page: 176

30. In which of the following sedimentary rocks would it be easiest to determine the type of rocks from which the sediment was derived?
    A) conglomerates   B) sandstones   C) shales   D) siltstones
    Ans: A   Page: 177

31. Which of the following types of sandstones is most likely to form by the rapid mechanical weathering of a granite?
    A) arkose   B) graywacke   C) quartz arenite   D) shale
    Ans: A   Page: 178

Use the following to answer question 32:

= quartz grains
= feldspar grains
= rock fragments
— clay matrix

scale
5 mm

32. What type of sandstone is depicted in the illustration above?
    A) arkose   B) graywacke   C) lithic sandstone   D) quartz arenite
    Ans: B   Page: 178

33. What type of sandstone contains abundant rock fragments?
    A) arkose   B) graywacke   C) lithic sandstone   D) quartz arenite
    Ans: C   Page: 178

34. Which of the following kinds of sandstone is the most poorly sorted?
    A) arkose   B) greywacke   C) lithic sandstone   D) quartz arenite
    Ans: B   Page: 178

35. The most abundant chemical/biochemical sedimentary rocks are _____.
    A) carbonates B) cherts C) sandstones D) shales
    Ans: A   Page: 179-180

36. Most of the carbonate sediments of the ocean are derived from _____.
    A) coral B) crustaceans C) fish D) foraminifera
    Ans: D   Page: 180

37. What is the most abundant non-clastic sediment?
    A) carbonate B) chert C) coal D) halite
    Ans: A   Page: 180

38. The Bahamas are an example of a(n) _____.
    A) alluvial environment B) carbonate platform C) deltaic deposit D) rift valley
    Ans: B   Page: 181

39. Where do atolls form?
    A) on beaches along active continental margins
    B) on subsiding volcanic islands
    C) on tidal flats in humid environments
    D) on wave-dominated deltas
    Ans: B   Page: 182-183

40. Which of the following minerals does not precipitate directly from seawater?
    A) calcite B) dolomite C) gypsum D) halite
    Ans: B   Page: 184

41. The conversion of limestone to dolostone involves the replacement of calcium ions with _____.
    A) carbonate ions B) magnesium ions C) silica ions D) sodium ions
    Ans: B   Page: 184

42. Which of the following is not a clastic sedimentary environment?
    A) alluvial B) beach C) deltaic D) evaporite
    Ans: D   Page: 182

43. Which of the following minerals is least likely to occur in a marine evaporite environment?
    A) calcite B) gypsum C) halite D) quartz
    Ans: D   Page: 185-186

44. Which of the following is deposited only by non-biological, chemical precipitation?
    A) chert B) coal C) halite D) limestone
    Ans: C   Page: 185-186

45. Which of the following minerals precipitates directly from water in evaporite deposits?
    A) dolomite   B) feldspar   C) gypsum   D) quartz
    Ans: C   Page: 186

46. Which of the following sedimentary rocks is composed of biochemically precipitated silica?
    A) chert   B) evaporite   C) limestone   D) quartz arenite
    Ans: A   Page: 186

47. Oil and gas are found mainly in _____.
    A) chert and gypsum   C) quartzite and dolomite
    B) mudstone and siltstone   D) sandstone and limestone
    Ans: D   Page: 187

48. Which of the following processes is not an important cause of subsidence during the development of a sedimentary basin?
    A) cooling and contraction of the crust   C) erosion of sediments
    B) deposition of sediments   D) tectonic downfaulting
    Ans: C   Page: 187

49. How thick are continental shelf deposits, such as the sedimentary deposits off of the east coast of the United States?
    A) 100 m   B) 1 km   C) 10 km   D) 100 km
    Ans: C   Page: 187

50. Which of the following types of sedimentary basins is most likely to develop where two plates collide?
    A) flexural basins
    B) rift basins
    C) thermal sag basins
    D) All of the above are equally likely to develop.
    Ans: A   Page: 189

Chapter 9: Metamorphic Rocks

1. Marble is a metamorphic rock that forms from _____?
   A) granite   B) limestone   C) sandstone   D) shale
   Ans: B   Page: 193

2. Which of the following tectonic settings will be coolest at 30 km depth?
   A)   regions of continental extension
   B)   stable continental lithosphere
   C)   volcanic arcs
   D)   The temperature in all three tectonic settings above will be the same at 30 km depth.
   Ans: B   Alternative Location: Online quizzing   Page: 194

3. Which of the following minerals is diagnostic of metamorphism?
   A) calcite   B) feldspar   C) staurolite   D) quartz
   Ans: C   Page: 193-194

4. What is the pressure on a rock at 15 kilometers depth in the Earth's crust?
   A)   approximately 4 times atmospheric pressure
   B)   approximately 40 times atmospheric pressure
   C)   approximately 400 times atmospheric pressure
   D)   approximately 4000 times atmospheric pressure
   Ans: D   Page: 195

5. A geothermometer is _____.
   A)   a device that measures current rock temperatures
   B)   a device that measures temperature when lowered into deep drill holes
   C)   a mineral assemblage that reveals the maximum temperature attained by a rock
   D)   the range of temperatures encountered by a rock in its geologic history
   Ans: C   Page: 195

6. What is the average rate at which temperature increases with depth in the Earth's crust?
   A) 10 °C/km   B) 30 °C/km   C) 100 °C/km   D) 300 °C/km
   Ans: B   Page: 195

7. Which of the following processes will cause metamorphism?
   A) an increase in pressure   C) interaction with hydrothermal fluids
   B) an increase in temperature   D) all of the above
   Ans: D   Page: 194

8. During metamorphism, changes in the bulk composition of a rock occur primarily as a result of _____.
   A) increases in pressure
   B) increases in temperature
   C) reaction with hydrothermal fluids
   D) <u>all</u> of the above
   Ans: C   Page: 195-196

9. Which of the following is a general pressure in all directions, such as the pressure that the atmosphere exerts?
   A) confining pressure
   B) directional pressure
   C) pore pressure
   D) stress pressure
   Ans: A   Page: 196

10. What is metasomatism?
    A) a change in the bulk composition of a rock during metamorphism
    B) metamorphism caused by nearby magmatic intrusions
    C) metamorphism caused by tectonic movements along faults
    D) the parallel alignment of minerals in a metamorphic rock
    Ans: A   Page: 196

11. What is the primary source of the carbon dioxide in metamorphic fluids?
    A) atmospheric carbon
    B) carbon dioxide released from Earth's core
    C) sedimentary carbonates
    D) weathered cement and other man-made materials
    Ans: C   Page: 196

12. What type of metamorphism is caused by high temperature and high pressure imposed over a large volume of crust?
    A) burial   B) contact   C) regional   D) shock
    Ans: C   Page: 197

13. What type of metamorphism is caused by igneous intrusions?
    A) burial metamorphism
    B) contact metamorphism
    C) regional metamorphism
    D) shock metamorphism
    Ans: B   Page: 197-198

14. At what depth does low-grade metamorphism begin?
    A) 1-2 km   B) 5-10 km   C) 20-50 km   D) 100-200 km
    Ans: B   Page: 198

15. Where does sea-floor metamorphism take place?
    A) continent collision zones
    B) divergent plate boundaries
    C) subduction zones
    D) transform plate boundaries
    Ans: B   Page: 199

16. What is the relation between metamorphic foliation and sedimentary bedding?
    A) Sedimentary bedding is generally perpendicular to metamorphic foliation.
    B) Sedimentary bedding is generally at a 45 degree angle to metamorphic foliation.
    C) Sedimentary bedding is generally parallel to metamorphic foliation.
    D) There is <u>no</u> general angular relationship between sedimentary bedding and metamorphic foliation.
    Ans: D   Page: 199

17. The parallel alignment of mica in a metamorphic rock is an example of _____.
    A) bedding   B) foliation   C) metasomatism   D) porphyroblasts
    Ans: B   Page: 199

18. What type of metamorphic rock was once used to make blackboards because of its ability to split easily into thin sheets along smooth, parallel surfaces?
    A) hornfels   B) quartzite   C) schist   D) slate
    Ans: D   Page: 199

19. Which of the following rocks represents the highest metamorphic grade?
    A) gneiss   B) phyllite   C) schist   D) slate
    Ans: A   Page: 200-201

20. Which of the following is <u>not</u> used to classify foliated rocks?
    A) the metamorphic grade   C) the size of the crystals
    B) the nature of the foliation   D) the texture of the parent rock
    Ans: D   Page: 199-202

21. Which of the following tectonic settings may be characterized by regional, high-pressure, and ultra-high pressure metamorphism?
    A) convergent plate boundaries   C) plate interiors
    B) divergent plate boundaries   D) transform plate boundaries
    Ans: A   Page: 199

22. Which of the following statements about the metamorphism of a shale is <u>false</u>?
    A) With increasing metamorphism, clay minerals break down to form micas.
    B) With increasing metamorphism, the grain size of the rock gets smaller.
    C) With increasing metamorphism, foliation develops.
    D) With increasing metamorphism, the amount of water in the rock decreases.
    Ans: B   Page: 200

23. Which of the following sequences describes the metamorphic changes in a shale with <u>increasing</u> metamorphic grade?
    A) schist → gneiss → slate   C) slate → schist → gneiss
    B) gneiss →slate → schist   D) gneiss → schist → slate
    Ans: C   Page: 200

24. Light-colored rocks with coarse bands of segregated light and dark minerals are called
_____.
A) gneisses   B) quartzites   C) schists   D) slates
Ans: A   Page: 200-201

25. Which of the following metamorphic rocks is <u>incorrectly</u> paired with its parent rock?
A) greenstone — basalt   C) quartzite — granite
B) marble — limestone   D) schist — shale
Ans: C   Page: 201-202

26. Which of the following metamorphic rocks is always foliated?
A) hornfels   B) marbles   C) quartzites   D) schists
Ans: D   Page: 202

27. Which of the following rocks has a granular texture?
A) gneiss   B) hornfels   C) schist   D) slate
Ans: B   Page: 202

28. Which of the following metamorphic rocks forms from mafic volcanic rocks?
A) greenstone   B) marble   C) quartzite   D) <u>all</u> of the above
Ans: A   Page: 202

29. A non-foliated contact metamorphic rock is called a _____.
A) gneiss   B) hornfels   C) phyllite   D) schist
Ans: B   Page: 201-202

30. Which of the following minerals would generally <u>not</u> be present in a granoblastic rock?
A) calcite   B) garnet   C) muscovite   D) quartz
Ans: C   Page: 201

31. Which of the following metamorphic rocks <u>cannot</u> form from a shale?
A) hornfels   B) marble   C) schist   D) slate
Ans: B   Alternative Location: Online quizzing   Page: 202

32. What type of metamorphic rock has undergone partial melting?
A) hornfels   B) migmatite   C) schist   D) slate
Ans: B   Page: 201

33. Which of the following rocks can be considered gradational between an igneous and a metamorphic rock?
A) amphibolite   B) gneiss   C) migmatite   D) zeolite
Ans: C   Page: 201

34. Which of the following metamorphic minerals commonly forms porphyroblasts?
    A) amphibole   B) calcite   C) chlorite   D) garnet
    Ans: D   Page: 203

35. What is a porphyroblast?
    A)   a common type of copper ore deposit
    B)   an igneous rock with two distinct crystal sizes
    C)   a relatively large metamorphic mineral
    D)   a strongly foliated metamorphic rock
    Ans: C   Page: 202

36. Which of the following rocks represents the highest grade of metamorphosed mafic volcanic rocks?
    A) amphibolite   B) blueschist   C) greenschist   D) granulite
    Ans: D   Page: 202

37. What metamorphic facies occurs at temperatures of 400°C and pressures of 6 kilobars?
    A) granulite   B) greenschist   C) hornfels   D) zeolite
    Ans: B   Page: 205

Use the following to answer questions 38-41:

The following questions refer to the metamorphic map below:

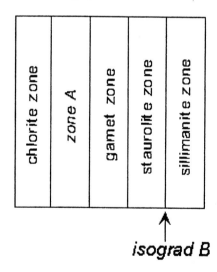

isograd B

38. In the figure above, what is *zone A*?
    A) biotite zone   B) kyanite zone   C) muscovite zone   D) quartz zone
    Ans: A   Page: 204

39. In the figure above, *isograd B* is the _____ isograd.
    A) garnet   B) mica   C) sillimanite   D) staurolite
    Ans: C   Page: 204

40. Based on the figure above, what mineral would <u>not</u> be present in garnet zone?
    A) biotite   B) chlorite   C) garnet   D) staurolite
    Ans: D   Page: 204-205

41. In the metamorphic map above, in which direction is the metamorphic grade increasing?
    A) east   B) north   C) south   D) west
    Ans: A   Page: 204-205

42. What is the most likely parent rock of a metamorphic rock containing muscovite, biotite, garnet, and quartz?
    A) basalt   B) limestone   C) sandstone   D) shale
    Ans: D   Page: 206

43. Which of the following metamorphic facies represents the highest temperature?
    A) amphibolite   B) blueschist   C) granulite   D) greenschist
    Ans: C   Page: 205-206

Use the following to answer questions 44-45:

The following questions refer to the diagram below.

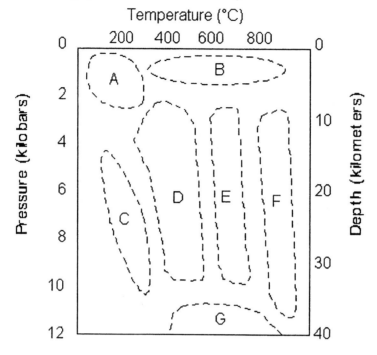

44. Which pressure-temperature regime represents the eclogite facies?
    A) area A   B) area C   C) area E   D) area G
    Ans: D   Page: 205

45. Which pressure-temperature regime represents the greenschist facies?
    A) area C   B) area D   C) area E   D) area F
    Ans: B   Page: 205

46. Under what conditions does zeolite-facies metamorphism occur?
    A)   relatively low pressure and low temperature
    B)   relatively low pressure and high temperature
    C)   relatively high pressure and low temperature
    D)   relatively high pressure and high temperature
    Ans: A   Page: 205

47. Which mineral is commonly used to determine a metamorphic P-T path?
    A) calcite   B) garnet   C) muscovite   D) quartz
    Ans: B   Page: 206

48. The prograde part of a metamorphic P-T path occurs during _____.
    A) burial and cooling   C) exhumation and cooling
    B) burial and heating   D) exhumation and heating
    Ans: B   Page: 206

49. Mélanges and blueschists are characteristic of which tectonic setting?
    A) continent collisions   C) subduction zones
    B) mid-ocean ridges   D) transform faults
    Ans: C   Page: 207

50. Which of the following metamorphic rocks forms in the forearc of a subduction zone?
    A) amphibolite   B) blueschist   C) hornfels   D) granulite
    Ans: B   Page: 207

Chapter 10: The Rock Record and the Geologic Time Scale

1. Historical records represent _____ of geologic time.
   A) less than 0.001%
   C) approximately 1%
   B) approximately 0.1%
   D) approximately 10%
   Ans: A   Page: 212

2. Which of the following is the best statement of the principle of original horizontality?
   A) Igneous intrusions form horizontal layers.
   B) Metamorphic isograds are horizontal before deformation.
   C) Sediments are deposited as horizontal layers.
   D) Most igneous, metamorphic, and sedimentary rocks in the Earth's crust form horizontal layers.
   Ans: C   Page: 215

3. An undeformed sedimentary layer is _____ than the layer above and _____ than the layer below.
   A) younger . . . younger
   C) older . . . younger
   B) younger . . . older
   D) older . . . older
   Ans: C   Page: 215

4. A stratigraphic succession is a vertical set of strata _____.
   A) bounded above and below by igneous and/or metamorphic rocks
   B) that is unique to a specific area
   C) that represents a repeating set of events, such as recurring floods and debris flows
   D) used as a chronological record of the geologic history of a region
   Ans: D   Page: 215

5. The principle of superposition states that _____.
   A) a fault is younger than the rocks it cuts
   B) sediments are deposited as essentially horizontal layers
   C) the present is the key to the past
   D) undisturbed sedimentary layers get progressively younger from bottom to top
   Ans: D   Page: 215

6. Which of the following is used by geologists to determine the relative ages in a rock sequence?
   A) cross-cutting relations   B) fossils   C) stratigraphy   D) all of the above
   Ans: D   Page: 215-220

7. The most common fossils in rocks of the last 500 million years are _____.
   A) invertebrate shells   B) leaves   C) vertebrate bones   D) vertebrate teeth
   Ans: A   Page: 216-217

8. Who proposed the theory of evolution?
   A) Leonardo da Vinci   C) William Smith
   B) Charles Darwin   D) Alfred Wegener
   Ans: B   Page: 217

9. Which of the following scientists is <u>incorrectly</u> paired with their major discovery?
   A) Henri Becquerel — radioactivity   C) James Hutton — rock cycle
   B) Charles Darwin — theory of evolution   D) Charles Lyell — faunal succession
   Ans: D   Page: 217-218

10. Fossils are most common in which rock types?
    A) igneous
    B) metamorphic
    C) sedimentary
    D) Fossils are equally common in sedimentary, igneous, and metamorphic rocks.
    Ans: C   Page: 217

11. The study of faunal succession allows _____.
    A) absolute dating of fossil-bearing strata
    B) correlation of marine fossils with modern mammals
    C) reconstruction of paleoclimates
    D) rocks to be correlated from different outcrops
    Ans: D   Page: 218

12. What is an unconformity?
    A) a gap in the geologic record
    B) a period of deposition
    C) a sedimentary layer of variable thickness
    D) a sequence of deformed rocks
    Ans: A   Page: 218

13. A disconformity is _____.
    A) an erosional surface between horizontal layers of sedimentary rocks
    B) an erosional surface between igneous and sedimentary rocks
    C) a rock unit that does not contain fossils
    D) a rock unit that is different than units above or below it
    Ans: A   Page: 219

14. Which of the following is an erosion surface that separates two sets of sedimentary layers with <u>non-parallel</u> bedding planes?
    A) angular unconformity   B) cross bed   C) disconformity   D) nonconformity
    Ans: A   Page: 219

15. In sequence stratigraphy, what is a sequence?
 A) a complete rock cycle C) a series of sedimentary beds
 B) a pattern of radioactive decay D) a set of common fossils
 Ans: D Page: 220

Use the following to answer questions 16-20:

The following questions refer to the geologic cross section below. Units A, B, C, D, E, and F are sedimentary rocks. Unit G is a granite.

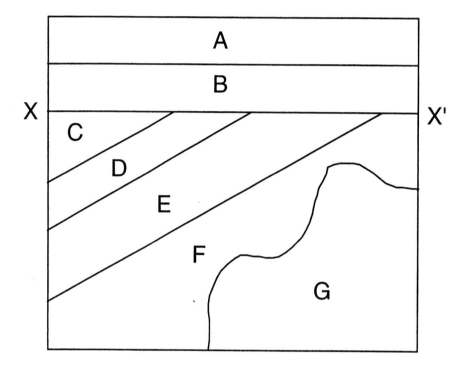

16. The horizontal line labeled X-X' is a(n) _____.
 A) angular unconformity B) contour C) cross bed D) fault
 Ans: A Page: 219

17. Which of the following units is the youngest?
 A) unit A B) unit B C) unit C D) unit F
 Ans: A Page: 218-219

18. Which of the following units is the oldest?
 A) unit A B) unit B C) unit C D) unit F
 Ans: D Page: 218-219

19. Which of the following events happened most recently?
    A) deposition of unit C
    B) deposition of unit D
    C) deposition of unit F
    D) tilting of units C, D, E, and F
    Ans: D   Page: 218-219

20. Which of the following statements is <u>true</u>?
    A) Deposition of unit A occurred before deposition of unit B.
    B) Erosion took place prior to deposition of unit B.
    C) Unit C is younger than unit A.
    D) The granite is older than unit F.
    Ans: B   Page: 218-219

Use the following to answer questions 21-23:

The following questions refer to the geologic cross section below. Units A, B, C, D, and E are sedimentary rocks. The thick dark line is a fault.

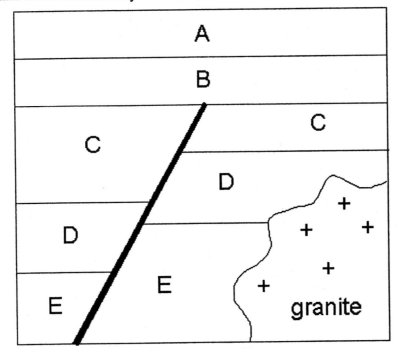

21. When did faulting occur?
    A) between the deposition of A and B
    B) between the deposition of B and C
    C) between the deposition of C and D
    D) between the deposition of D and E
    Ans: B   Page: 218-220

22. What is the relative timing between faulting and intrusion of the granite?
    A) Faulting occurred after the intrusion of the granite.
    B) Faulting occurred before the intrusion of the granite.
    C) Faulting and intrusion of the granite occurred at the same time.
    D) The relative timing between faulting and intrusion of the granite cannot be determined from the information provided.
    Ans: D   Page: 218-220

23. Which of the following units is the oldest?
    A) unit A   B) unit C   C) unit E   D) the granite
    Ans: C   Page: 218-220

24. Which of the following is the smallest division of geologic time?
    A) eons   B) epochs   C) eras   D) periods
    Ans: B   Page: 225

25. How old are the oldest rocks on Earth?
    A) approximately 10,000 years old
    B) approximately 65 million years old
    C) approximately 500 million years old
    D) approximately 4 billion years old
    Ans: D   Page: 221

26. How long did the Proterozoic Eon last?
    A) approximately 500 million years
    B) approximately 1 billion years
    C) approximately 2 billion years
    D) approximately 4 billion years
    Ans: C   Page: 222

27. When were the Earth's climate, geodynamo, and plate tectonics systems established?
    A) during the Archean
    B) during the Cenozoic
    C) during the Paleozoic
    D) during the Proterozoic
    Ans: A   Page: 224

28. During which geologic eon did the amount of oxygen in the atmosphere approach modern levels?
    A) during the Archean
    B) during the Hadean
    C) during the Phanerozoic
    D) during the Protorozoic
    Ans: D   Page: 221

29. When did the Mesozoic era begin?
    A) 65 million years ago
    B) 250 million years ago
    C) 543 million years ago
    D) 2.5 billion years ago
    Ans: B   Page: 224

Use the following to answer questions 30-33:

The following questions refer to the diagram below.

Phanerozoic													Proterozoic	Archean
Cenozoic		Mesozoic			Paleozoic									
Quaternary	Tertiary	Cretaceous	Jurassic	Triassic	Permian	Carbon-iferous (Mississippian / Pennsylvanian)		Devonian	Silurian	Ordovician	Cambrian		E	

A   B   C   D

30. What is the best estimate for the age of point C?
    A) 25 million years   C) 145 million years
    B) 65 million years   D) 250 million years
    Ans: D   Page: 224

31. What is the best estimate for the age of point E?
    A) 0.5 billion years   B) 1.5 billion years   C) 3.0 billion years   D) 4.5 billion years
    Ans: C   Page: 224

32. When did fossils of complex organisms (such as shells) first become abundant in the
    geologic record?
    A) at point B   B) at point C   C) at point D   D) at point E
    Ans: C   Page: 224-225

33. When did dinosaurs rule the Earth?
    A) between A and B   C) between C and D
    B) between B and C   D) between D and E
    Ans: B   Page: 232

34. When did the world's oil and gas reserves form?
    A) during the Archean   C) during the Phanerozoic
    B) during the Hadean   D) during the Proterozoic
    Ans: C   Page: 225

35. Which of the following statements about radioactivity is <u>false</u>?
    A) A radioactive element decays at a constant rate.
    B) Energy is consumed during radioactive decay.
    C) The decay product of a radioactive element is called the daughter product.
    D) Radioactivity is the spontaneous disintegration of the nucleus of an atom.
    Ans: B   Page: 225-228

36. Which of the following statements regarding radiometric dating is <u>true</u>?
    A) After two half-lives, no radioactive atoms remain.
    B) Carbon-14 cannot be used to date material more than 100,000 years old.
    C) Sedimentary rocks can be dated more easily than igneous rocks.
    D) The radioactive decay product is called the parent atom.
    Ans: B   Page: 225-230

37. What is the youngest rock formation exposed in the Grand Canyon?
    A) Bright Angel Shale   C) Redwall Limestone
    B) Kaibab Limestone   D) Vishnu Schist
    Ans: B   Page: 226-227

38. When did the oldest rocks, now exposed at the base of the Grand Canyon, form?
    A) during the Cenozoic   C) during the Paleozoic
    B) during the Mesozoic   D) during the Precambrian
    Ans: D   Page: 226-227

39. When did the horizontal, layered sedimentary rocks in the Grand Canyon form?
    A) during the Cenozoic   C) during the Paleozoic
    B) during the Mesozoic   D) <u>all</u> of the above
    Ans: C   Page: 226-227

40. Which of the following can change the rate of radioactive decay?
    A) changes in temperature   C) chemical reactions
    B) changes in pressure   D) <u>none</u> of the above
    Ans: D   Page: 228

41. A rock formed with 1000 atoms of a radioactive parent element, but contains only 250 radioactive parent atoms today. If the half-life for the radioactive element is one million years, how old is the rock?
    A) 250,000 years old   C) 2,000,000 years old
    B) 750,000 years old   D) 4,000,000 years old
    Ans: C   Page: 228

42. Which of the following instruments is used to precisely measure isotopes for radiometric dating?
    A) electron microprobe
    B) geiger counter
    C) mass spectrometer
    D) petrologic microscope
    Ans: C   Page: 228

43. Radiometric dating is least useful for dating _____ rocks.
    A) basaltic   B) granitic   C) metamorphic   D) sedimentary
    Ans: D   Page: 228-229

44. Which of the following radioactive isotopes has the shortest half-life?
    A) carbon-14   B) potassium-40   C) rubidium-87   D) uranium-238
    Ans: A   Page: 229

45. Radiometric dating is possible if a rock contains a measurable amount of _____.
    A) daughter atoms
    B) parent atoms
    C) both daughter <u>and</u> parent atoms
    D) either daughter <u>or</u> parent atoms
    Ans: C   Page: 229

46. Which of the following radioactive isotopes is the most useful for dating very young (<10,000 years old) wood and charcoal?
    A) carbon-14   B) potassium-40   C) rubidium-87   D) uranium-238
    Ans: A   Page: 229

47. Which of the following materials might be dated using carbon-14?
    A) granite   B) iron ore   C) sandstone   D) wood
    Ans: D   Page: 229

48. Approximately how fast do plates spread apart?
    A) 1 to 10 millimeters per year
    B) 2 to 20 centimeters per year
    C) 5 to 25 meters per year
    D) 3 to 10 kilometers per year
    Ans: B   Page: 230

49. If the Earth's history was compressed into a single calendar year, complex organisms (including those with shells) first appeared in _____.
    A) February   B) June   C) October   D) December
    Ans: C   Page: 233

50. Human beings (*homo sapiens*) evolved during which geologic era?
    A) Cenozoic   B) Mesozoic   C) Paleozoic   D) Precambrian
    Ans: A   Page: 232

Chapter 11: Folds, Faults and Other Records of Rock Deformation

1. The line formed by the intersection of an inclined sedimentary layer and a horizontal plane is called the _____.
   A) bed   B) dip   C) fold axis   D) strike
   Ans: D   Page: 238-239

2. The dip of a unit represents the _____.
   A) angle at which the bed inclines from the horizontal
   B) direction of intersection of the rock layer and a horizontal surface
   C) part of the unit that has been eroded
   D) tilt of the rock unit before deformation
   Ans: A   Page: 239

3. Which of the following types of tectonic forces tends to squeeze and shorten a rock body?
   A) compressive forces   C) tensional forces
   B) shearing forces   D) all of the above
   Ans: A   Page: 240

4. Which of the following types of tectonic forces tends to push two sides of a body in opposite directions so that they slide horizontally past one another?
   A) compressive forces   C) tensional forces
   B) shearing forces   D) torsional forces
   Ans: B   Page: 240

Use the following to answer question 5:

5. What type of fault is depicted in the cross section above?
   A) left-lateral strike-slip fault
   B) normal fault
   C) reverse fault
   D) right-lateral strike-slip fault
   Ans: B   Page: 245

6. Which of the following statements best describes the behavior of rocks during deformation?
   A) Brittle materials deform by faulting, whereas ductile materials deform by folding.
   B) Brittle materials deform by folding, whereas ductile materials deform by faulting.
   C) Both brittle and ductile materials deform by faulting.
   D) Both brittle and ductile materials deform by folding.
   Ans: A   Page: 242

7. What type of material undergoes smooth, continuous plastic deformation?
   A) brittle   B) cataclastic   C) ductile   D) all of the above
   Ans: C   Page: 242

8. What type of forces dominate at convergent plate margins?
   A) compressive forces
   B) shearing forces
   C) tensional forces
   D) torsional forces
   Ans: A   Page: 242

9. The San Andreas Fault is a result of what type of forces?
   A) compressive forces
   B) shearing forces
   C) tensional forces
   D) all of the above
   Ans: B   Page: 243

10. Confining pressure is pressure applied _____.
    A) along a diagonal plane
    B) along a horizontal plane
    C) along a vertical plane
    D) in all directions
    Ans: D   Page: 242

11. Which of the following statements about rock deformation is <u>false</u>?
    A) Deep crustal rocks are more likely to deform ductilely than shallow crustal rocks.
    B) Hotter rocks are more likely to deform ductilely than cooler rocks.
    C) Most sedimentary rocks are more deformable than igneous rocks.
    D) Rocks under low confining pressure are more likely to deform ductilely than rocks under high confining pressure.
    Ans: D   Page: 242

12. What determines whether a rock deforms in a brittle fashion versus a ductile fashion?
    A) temperature
    B) pressure
    C) rock type
    D) temperature, pressure, <u>and</u> rock type
    Ans: D   Page: 242

13. If a basalt unit near the surface of the Earth underwent compressive deformation, the result would most likely be _____.
    A) folding
    B) faulting
    C) folding followed by faulting
    D) faulting followed by folding
    Ans: B   Page: 242

14. A sample of marble has deformed brittlely during a laboratory experiment. If we wish our next sample of marble to deform plastically rather than brittlely, we should conduct the next experiment at _____.
    A) lower temperature and lower confining pressure
    B) lower temperature and higher confining pressure
    C) higher temperature and lower confining pressure
    D) higher temperature and higher confining pressure
    Ans: D   Page: 242

15. Which of the following conditions of natural deformation is the most difficult to simulate in a laboratory experiment?
    A) the duration of the deformation event
    B) the pressure during the deformation event
    C) the temperature during the deformation event
    D) the type of rock that was deformed
    Ans: A   Page: 242

16. What is the scientific term for a crack along which no appreciable movement has occurred?
    A) axis   B) fault   C) fold   D) joint
    Ans: D   Page: 243

17. The difference between a fault and a joint is that _____.
   A) faults cut through more than one layer of rock, whereas joints cut through only one layer
   B) faults cut through bedrock, whereas joints cut only the upper sedimentary layers
   C) rocks on either side of a fault have moved, whereas rocks on either side of a joint have remained stationary
   D) faults form straight lines in map view, whereas joints form zigzag lines
   Ans: C   Page: 243

18. Which of the following deformation textures forms deep in the Earth's crust?
   A) cataclastic textures   B) fault breccias   C) joints   D) mylonites
   Ans: D   Page: 243

19. The San Andreas fault is an example of a _____ fault.
   A) normal   B) reverse   C) right-lateral strike-slip   D) left-lateral strike-slip
   Ans: C   Page: 245

20. Which of the following is not a dip-slip fault?
   A) a normal fault   B) a reverse fault   C) a right-lateral fault   D) a thrust fault
   Ans: C   Page: 245

21. Reverse faults form in response to _____ forces.
   A) compressive   B) shearing   C) tensional   D) torsional
   Ans: A   Page: 245

22. What type of fault is characterized by the rocks above the fault plane moving downward, relative to the rocks below the fault plane?
   A) a normal fault   B) a reverse fault   C) a strike-slip fault   D) all of the above
   Ans: A   Page: 245

23. A fault plane strikes north-south and dips steeply to the west. Geologic observations indicate that most of the fault movement was vertical and that Mesozoic rocks occur east of the fault and Paleozoic rocks occur west of the fault. What type of fault is this?
   A) a left-lateral fault   B) a normal fault   C) a reverse fault   D) a right-lateral fault
   Ans: C   Page: 245

24. An oblique-slip fault suggests _____ .
   A) compressive forces only
   B) shear forces only
   C) tensional forces only
   D) shear forces combined with compressive or tensional forces
   Ans: D   Page: 245

25. What is a thrust fault?
   A) a low-angle normal fault
   B) a low-angle oblique fault
   C) a low-angle reverse fault
   D) a low-angle strike-slip fault
   Ans: C   Page: 245

26. Which of the following correctly links the tectonic force with the expected type of faulting?
   A) compression = normal faulting
   B) shear = strike-slip faulting
   C) tension = reverse faulting
   D) tension + compression = oblique-slip faulting
   Ans: B   Page: 245

27. The total amount of shortening in an overthrust may exceed several _____.
   A) meters   B) tens of meters   C) hundreds of meters   D) kilometers
   Ans: D   Page: 245

28. Which of the following types of tectonic forces causes faulting?
   A) compressive forces   B) shear forces   C) tensional forces   D) all of the above
   Ans: D   Page: 245

29. What two measurements describe the orientation of a fault plane at a given location?
   A) axis and plane   B) dip and strike   C) lateral and thrust   D) plunge and trend
   Ans: B   Page: 245

30. What type of tectonic forces formed the Keystone thrust fault in southern Nevada?
   A) compressive forces
   B) shearing forces
   C) tensional forces
   D) all of the above
   Ans: A   Page: 246

31. A rift valley is _____.
   A) a downfaulted block
   B) an eroded dome
   C) an eroded basin
   D) an upfaulted block
   Ans: A   Page: 246

32. Which of the following geologic features is formed in a region deformed by tensional tectonic forces?
   A) an anticline   B) a thrust fault   C) a strike-slip fault   D) a rift valley
   Ans: D   Page: 246-247

33. In an anticline, _____.
    A) the oldest rocks occur in the center and the limbs dip toward the center
    B) the oldest rocks occur in the center and the limbs dip away from the center
    C) the youngest rocks occur in the center and the limbs dip toward the center
    D) the youngest rocks occur in the center and the limbs dip away from the center
    Ans: B   Page: 248

34. The surface that divides a fold into two symmetrical halves is called the _____.
    A) axial plane   B) fault   C) fold axis   D) limb
    Ans: A   Page: 248

35. Upfolds, or arches, of layered rock are called _____.
    A) anticlines   B) faults   C) synclines   D) unconformities
    Ans: A   Page: 248

36. Which of the following statements about synclines is true?
    A) The oldest rocks occur in the center and the limbs dip toward the center.
    B) The oldest rocks occur in the center and the limbs dip away from the center.
    C) The youngest rocks occur in the center and the limbs dip toward the center.
    D) The youngest rocks occur in the center and the limbs dip away from the center.
    Ans: C   Page: 248

Use the following to answer questions 37-40:

The following questions refer to the geologic map below. Units A, B, and C are sedimentary rocks; unit A is the oldest and unit C is the youngest. The sedimentary rocks are cut by a fault, indicated by the bold line. The fault dips 60° to the northwest as shown by the strike and dip symbol.

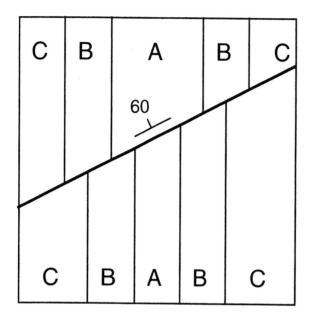

37. What type of structure is shown in the geologic map?
   A) a faulted anticline
   B) a faulted syncline
   C) a folded strike-slip fault
   D) The structure <u>cannot</u> be determined from the information given.
   Ans: A   Page: 248

38. Which way do the sedimentary layers dip?
   A) toward the east   C) toward the center
   B) toward the west   D) toward the east and west
   Ans: D   Page: 248

39. Why is unit A wider north of the fault than it is south of the fault?
   A) Deeper levels of the structure are exposed on the north side of the fault.
   B) Erosion has removed most of unit A south of the fault.
   C) Faulting has thinned unit A south of the fault.
   D) Unit A had a variable thickness prior to faulting.
   Ans: A   Page: 248

40. What type of fault is depicted on the geologic map?
    A) a normal fault   B) a reverse fault   C) a right-lateral fault   D) a left-lateral fault
    Ans: B   Page: 245

41. An overturned fold is characterized by two limbs _____.
    A) at right angles to one another
    B) dipping in the same direction, with one limb tilted beyond vertical
    C) dipping steeply in opposite directions
    D) dipping gently in opposite directions
    Ans: B   Page: 248-249

42. If sedimentary rocks on a geologic map form a zigzag pattern, the underlying structure
    probably consists of _____.
    A) domes and basins   C) intersecting joint sets
    B) horizontal anticlines and synclines D) plunging anticlines and synclines
    Ans: C   Page: 249-250

43. What type of structure is characterized by rock layers that dip radially toward a central
    point?
    A) an anticline   B) a basin   C) a dome   D) a syncline
    Ans: B   Page: 250

44. Older rocks crop out in the core of which of the structures listed below?
    I. anticline   II. syncline   III. dome   IV. basin
    A) structures I and II   C) structures I and III
    B) structures III and IV   D) structures II and IV
    Ans: C   Page: 248-251

45. Oil is commonly trapped in _____.
    A) structural basins   B) structural domes   C) synclines   D) all of the above
    Ans: B   Page: 250-251

Use the following to answer questions 46-47:

The following questions refer to the block diagram below.

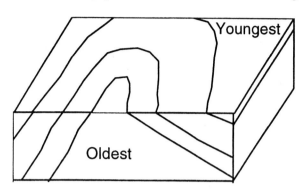

46. The structure shown in the diagram above is a(n) _____.
    A) anticline   B) basin   C) dome   D) syncline
    Ans: A   Page: 248-250

47. The structure shown in the diagram above is a _____.
    A) horizontal, symmetric fold   C) plunging, symmetric fold
    B) horizontal, asymmetric fold   D) plunging, asymmetric fold
    Ans: D   Page: 248-250

48. Oil can be trapped at the top of a dome if _____.
    A) there is a nearby basin
    B) there is an impermeable layer at the top of the dome
    C) the dome has been eroded
    D) the dome is part of an adjoining syncline
    Ans: B   Page: 250

49. Where do basins form?
    A) where a part of the crust has been heated and subsequently cools and contracts
    B) where tensional forces stretch the crust
    C) where thick sequences of sediment are deposited
    D) all of the above
    Ans: D   Page: 250-251

50. If erosion stripped the top off a dome, one would find _____.
    A) the oldest rocks exposed in the center
    B) the youngest rocks exposed in the center
    C) a linear pattern of rock outcrops
    D) A and C
    Ans: A   Page: 251

Chapter 12: Mass Wasting

1. Which of the following statements is <u>false</u>?
   A) Mass movements occur when the force of gravity exceeds the strength of the slope materials.
   B) Mass movements can be triggered by earthquakes and floods.
   C) Materials can move down a slope very slowly or as a sudden, catastrophic, large movement.
   D) Mass movements require wind or running water.
   Ans: D   Page: 257

2. Which of the following processes describes the general downhill movement of rock, soil, or unconsolidated materials under the influence of gravity?
   A) debris sliding   B) mass wasting   C) surface tension   D) weathering
   Ans: B   Page: 258

3. Which of the following forces is the dominant cause of mass movement?
   A) gravity   B) seismic energy   C) tidal force   D) wind
   Ans: A   Page: 258

4. Which of the following is <u>not</u> an important factor in causing mass movements?
   A) amount of water in materials   C) steepness and instability of slopes
   B) nature of slope materials   D) temperature of slope materials
   Ans: D   Page: 258

5. Which of the following would be most likely to undergo liquefaction?
   A) granite   B) talus slope   C) unconsolidated soil   D) water-saturated sand
   Ans: D   Page: 259

6. A hill consisting of loose, dry sand that slopes at the angle of repose and has no vegetation _____.
   A) is stable unless oversteepened by excavation
   B) may flow if it becomes saturated with water
   C) will be more stable if vegetation takes root on the hill
   D) <u>all</u> of the above
   Ans: D   Page: 259-262

7. Which of the following statements is <u>true</u>?
   A) Fine sand forms steeper slopes than coarse sand.
   B) Angular pebbles form steeper slopes than coarse sand.
   C) Water-saturated sand forms steeper slopes than dry sand.
   D) Dry debris forms steeper slopes than damp debris.
   Ans: B   Page: 259-260

8. The angle of repose does <u>not</u> depend upon which of the following?
   A) particle composition   B) particle shape   C) particle size   D) water content
   Ans: A   Page: 259

9. Which of the following has the steepest angle of repose?
   A) dry sand   C) water-saturated sand
   B) damp sand   D) water over-saturated sand
   Ans: B   Page: 259-260

Use the following to answer question 10:

10. The illustration above depicts a cross section through a pile of quartz sand. The angle depicted in the diagram is called the _____.
    A) angle of repose   B) bedding angle   C) cleavage angle   D) dip
    Ans: A   Page: 259-260

Use the following to answer question 11:

11. The illustration above most likely depicts a cross section through a pile of _____.
    A) dry sand   C) water-saturated sand
    B) damp sand   D) water-oversaturated sand
    Ans: B   Page: 259-260

12. The property by which a paper clip can float on the surface of a liquid is called
    _____.
    A) cohesion   B) liquefaction   C) solifluction   D) surface tension
    Ans: D   Page: 259

13. A paper clip can float on the surface of a liquid because the molecules _____.
    A) in the interior of the liquid have a net inward attraction
    B) in the interior of the liquid have a net outward attraction
    C) at the surface of the liquid have a net inward attraction
    D) at the surface of the liquid have a net outward attraction
    Ans: C   Page: 260

14. Surface tension is greatest when sand is _____.
    A) dry   C) saturated with water
    B) damp, but not saturated with water   D) oversaturated with water
    Ans: B   Page: 259-260

15. As the amount of water in a pile of quartz sand increases, the angle of repose will

    _____.
    A) increase   B) decrease   C) first increase and then decrease   D) not change
    Ans: C   Page: 259-260

16. What is the angle of repose of dry, coarse sand?
    A) about 20°   B) about 40°   C) about 60°   D) about 80°
    Ans: B   Page: 259-260

17. Which of the following has the steepest angle of repose?
    A) angular quartz pebbles
    B) coarse quartz sand
    C) fine quartz sand
    D) All of the above have the same angle of repose.
    Ans: A   Page: 259-260

18. Which of the following slopes of unconsolidated material will be the least stable?
    A) a slope less than the angle of repose   C) a slope greater than the angle of repose
    B) a slope equal to the angle of repose   D) All of the above will be equally stable.
    Ans: C   Page: 261

19. Which of the following situations is most likely to undergo mass wasting?
    A) a dry, moderate slope of unconsolidated material
    B) a wet, moderate slope of unconsolidated material
    C) a dry, steep slope of unconsolidated material
    D) a wet, steep slope of unconsolidated material
    Ans: D   Page: 261

20. Stripping soil of vegetation by burning or deforestation will _____ the likelihood of
    mass movements.
    A) greatly decrease   B) decrease   C) not affect   D) increase
    Ans: D   Page: 261-262

Use the following to answer questions 21-22:

The following questions refer to the cross section through the upper part of the Grand Canyon depicted below:

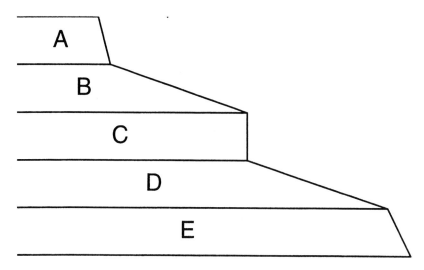

21. Which of the following rocks most likely makes up units B and D?
   A) granite   B) limestone   C) sandstone   D) shale
   Ans: D   Page: 261

22. Unit C is most likely composed of _____.
   A) sandstone   B) shale   C) unconsolidated sediments   D) volcanic ash
   Ans: A   Page: 261

23. In the United States economic losses from landslides each year are approximately

   _____.
   A) $100-200,000   B) $1-2 million   C) $1-2 billion   D) $1-2 trillion
   Ans: C   Page: 262

24. Which of the following statements best describes the results of the Japanese government's investment in landslide control programs that began in 1958?
   A) The programs have significantly decreased the number of people killed and the number of homes destroyed by landslides.
   B) The programs have helped slightly, but the increase in Japan's population has resulted in more people being killed by landslides.
   C) The programs have not significantly decreased the number of people killed and homes destroyed by landslides.
   D) The programs have actually slightly increased the number of people killed and homes destroyed by landslides.
   Ans: A   Page: 262-263

25. Which of the following slopes is <u>least</u> stable?
    A) a slope where the sedimentary layers dip parallel to the slope
    B) a slope where the sedimentary layers are horizontal
    C) a slope where the sedimentary layers dip perpendicular to the slope
    D) <u>All</u> of these slopes have the same stability.
    Ans: A   Page: 261-260

26. Which of the following processes was the major reason so many landslides occurred during the 1964 Anchorage, Alaska earthquake?
    A) Motion along the fault oversteepened slopes.
    B) Water-saturated sandy layers became liquefied during the earthquake.
    C) The earthquake tilted the rock layers downhill.
    D) The earthquake caused water to accumulate in the soil.
    Ans: B   Page: 263

27. The accumulation of rocks at the base of a cliff is called _____.
    A) a dune   B) an alluvial fan   C) soil creep   D) talus
    Ans: D   Page: 265

28. In what class of mass movement does the material move as if it were a fluid?
    A) creeps   B) falls   C) flows   D) slides
    Ans: C   Page: 264

29. What is the difference between a rockslide and a rock avalanche?
    A) In a rockslide, the rocks move more or less as a unit, whereas in a rock avalanche the rocks move independently like a fluid.
    B) In a rockslide, the rocks move independently like a fluid, whereas in a rock avalanche the rocks move more or less as a unit.
    C) A rockslide is faster than a rock avalanche.
    D) A rockslide involves more debris than a rock avalanche.
    Ans: A   Page: 265-266

Use the following to answer questions 30-33:

The following questions refer to the table below:

Dominant material	Nature of motion	Slow (1 cm/yr)	Moderate (1 km/hr)	Fast (5 km/hr)
Rock	Flow	a	b	c
Rock	Slide or fall	d	e	f
Unconsolidated	Flow	g	h	i
Unconsolidated	Slide or fall	j	k	l

30. How would a slump be classified in the table above?
    A) box *a* B) box *d* C) box *g* D) box *j*
    Ans: D   Page: 265

31. How would a mudflow be classified in the table above?
    A) box *a* B) box *b* C) box *g* D) box *h*
    Ans: D   Page: 265

32. How would soil creep be classified in the table above?
    A) box *g* B) box *h* C) box *j* D) box *k*
    Ans: A   Page: 265

33. How would a rock avalanche be classified in the table above?
    A) box *b* B) box *c* C) box *e* D) box *f*
    Ans: B   Page: 265

34. Which of the following types of mass movements could a person <u>not</u> outrun?
    A) debris avalanche B) earth flow C) slump D) soil creep
    Ans: A   Page: 265, 268

35. A slow slide of unconsolidated material that travels as a unit is called _____.
    A) a debris flow B) a rockslide C) a slump D) soil creep
    Ans: C   Page: 265, 269

36. Which of the following types of mass movement has the greatest air content?
    A) debris flow B) rock avalanche C) rockslide D) slump
    Ans: B   Page: 265

37. Telephone poles that lean slightly downhill are a likely result of which of the following processes?
    A) creep B) debris slide C) earthflow D) rock avalanche
    Ans: A   Page: 267-268

38. Which of the following types of mass movements consists of relatively fine-grained material?
    A) debris flows B) earthflows C) rock avalanches D) rockslides
    Ans: B   Page: 268

39. What is the difference between an earthflow and a debris flow?
    A) Earthflows consist of consolidated rock; mudflows consist of unconsolidated material.
    B) Earthflows travel faster than debris flows.
    C) Earthflows consist of finer material than debris flows.
    D) Earthflows contain more rock fragments than debris flows.
    Ans: C   Page: 268

40. Which of the following statements about mudflows is <u>false</u>?
    A) Mudflows tend to move slower than debris flows.
    B) Mudflows are most common in semi-arid regions.
    C) Mudflows contain large amounts of water.
    D) Mudflows can carry large boulders.
    Ans: A   Page: 268

41. Which of the following would be the most destructive mass movement?
    A) slump B) debris slide C) solifluction D) debris avalanche
    Ans: D   Page: 269-270

42. Which of the following processes only occurs in permafrost regions?
    A) landsliding B) liquefaction C) soil creep D) solifluction
    Ans: D   Page: 268

43. Why are debris avalanches and mudflows common on volcanic slopes?
    A) because there is abundant unconsolidated volcanic ash
    B) because earthquakes associated with volcanic eruptions trigger mass movements
    C) because volcanic eruptions trigger melting of ice and snow
    D) <u>all</u> of the above
    Ans: D   Page: 269

44. A slump is _____.
    A) a rock flow   C) a flow of unconsolidated material
    B) a rock slide   D) a slide of unconsolidated material
    Ans: D   Page: 269

45. Which of the following statements best describes a slump?
    A) slow downhill movement of unconsolidated material moving as a unit
    B) slow downhill movement of unconsolidated material moving like a fluid
    C) rapid downhill movement of unconsolidated material moving as a unit
    D) rapid downhill movement of unconsolidated material moving like a fluid
    Ans: A   Page: 270

46. Why are few mass movements preserved in the geologic record?
    A) Mass movement deposits are destroyed by diagenesis.
    B) Mass movement deposits erode easily.
    C) Mass movements have only occurred recently owing to human activities.
    D) Mass movements were rare in the past owing to low rainfall.
    Ans: B   Page: 270

47. Which of the following may be triggered by submarine slides?
    A) earthquakes   B) liquifaction   C) tsunamis   D) all of the above
    Ans: C   Page: 270

48. Which of the following was not a contributing factor in the 1925 Gros Ventre slide near Jackson Hole, Wyoming?
    A) undercutting of the slope by construction activities
    B) slippery bedding planes in a shale unit
    C) the orientation of the sedimentary layers with respect to the slope
    D) All of these were contributing factors.
    Ans: D   Page: 271-272

49. Mass movements would least likely occur in which of the following settings?
    A) ocean-continent convergence zones   C) intraplate settings
    B) divergent plate boundaries   D) ocean-ocean convergence zones
    Ans: C   Page: 273

50. Which of the following major landslides was caused, in part, by human activities?
    A) the 1925 Gros Ventre landslide near Jackson Hole, Wyoming
    B) the 1963 Vaiont landslide in the Italian Alps
    C) the 1983 Spanish Fork Canyon landslide, Utah
    D) the Nevado Huascaran ice-debris avalanche, Peruvian Andes
    Ans: B   Page: 273

Chapter 13: The Hydrologic Cycle and Groundwater

1. After oceans, which of the following reservoirs contains the most water?
   A) atmosphere
   B) glaciers and polar ice
   C) lakes and rivers
   D) underground waters
   Ans: B   Page: 278

2. Which of the following reservoirs contains the least water?
   A) atmosphere   B) biosphere   C) groundwater   D) lakes and rivers
   Ans: B   Page: 278

3. The process by which surface water becomes groundwater is called _____.
   A) discharge   B) evaporation   C) infiltration   D) transpiration
   Ans: C   Page: 278

4. What powers the hydrologic cycle?
   A) magnetism   B) mantle convection   C) radioactive decay   D) solar energy
   Ans: D   Page: 278

5. With respect to the Earth's land surface, which of the following mathematical balances is correct?
   A) precipitation = evaporation – runoff
   B) precipitation = runoff – evaporation
   C) precipitation = evaporation + runoff
   D) precipitation = evaporation × runoff
   Ans: C   Page: 279

6. The release of water vapor from plants is called _____.
   A) evaporation   B) infiltration   C) precipitation   D) transpiration
   Ans: D   Page: 278

7. Which of the following terms is a measure of the amount of water vapor in the air as a proportion of the maximum amount the air could hold at the same temperature?
   A) dew point   B) evaporation rate   C) relative humidity   D) sublimation point
   Ans: C   Page: 280-281

Use the following to answer question 8:

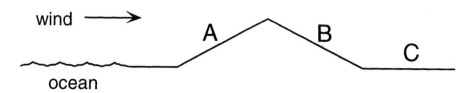

wind ⟶   A   B   C

ocean

8. The diagram above represents a cross section through a coastal mountain range. Which of the following statements is correct?
   A) Region A would receive the most precipitation.
   B) Region B would receive the most precipitation.
   C) Region C would receive the most precipitation.
   D) Regions A, B, and C would receive about the same amount of precipitation.
   Ans: A   Page: 281

9. Which of the following regions has the highest average annual precipitation?
   A) northeast United States   C) southwest United States
   B) southeast United States   D) central United States
   Ans: B   Page: 282

10. What is the average annual precipitation in Phoenix, Arizona [*substitute your city, state here*]?
    A) less than 20 cm   B) 20-40 cm   C) 40-60 cm   D) more than 60 cm
    Ans: A   Page: 282

11. Which of the following regions has the highest annual surface runoff?
    A) central Texas   C) southern Florida
    B) northern Michigan   D) western Washington
    Ans: D   Page: 282

12. Which of the following rivers carries the most water?
    A) the Amazon River in South America   C) the Ganges River in Asia
    B) the Congo River in Africa   D) the Mississippi River in North America
    Ans: A   Page: 283

13. In the United States, what percentage of the original wetlands has been destroyed?
    A) less than 5%   B) about 10%   C) about 25%   D) more than 50%
    Ans: D   Page: 284

14. Groundwater represents how much of the world's fresh water?
    A) about 1%   B) about 5%   C) about 20%   D) about 50%
    Ans: C   Page: 284

15. Layers that transmit groundwater are called _____.
    A) aquicludes   B) aquifers   C) influent streams   D) unsaturated zones
    Ans: B   Page: 284

16. Which of the following unfractured rocks has the highest porosity?
    A) granite   B) sandstone   C) schist   D) shale
    Ans: B   Page: 284-285

17. Which of the following statements regarding porosity and permeability is true?
    A) High porosity rocks generally have high permeability.
    B) High porosity rocks generally have low permeability.
    C) Low porosity rocks generally have high permeability.
    D) Porosity and permeability have identical meanings.
    Ans: A   Page: 285

18. Which of the following sandstones will have the highest porosity?
    A) a poorly sorted, cemented sandstone   C) a well sorted, cemented sandstone
    B) a poorly sorted, uncemented sandstone D) a well sorted, uncemented sandstone
    Ans: D   Page: 284-285

19. Permeability is the _____.
    A) ability of a solid to allow fluids to pass through
    B) amount of water vapor in the air relative to the maximum amount of water vapor the
        air can hold
    C) percentage of pore space in a rock
    D) process by which plants release water vapor to the atmosphere
    Ans: A   Page: 285

20. In the unsaturated zone, pore spaces in the soil and rock contain _____.
    A) air   B) water   C) air and water   D) neither air nor water
    Ans: C   Page: 285-286

21. Which of the following combinations make for the best groundwater reservoir?
    A) low permeability and low porosity   C) high permeability and low porosity
    B) low permeability and high porosity   D) high permeability and high porosity
    Ans: D   Page: 285

22. What is the difference between the saturated and unsaturated zones of groundwater?
    A) The saturated zone has a higher porosity than the unsaturated zone.
    B) The saturated zone has a lower porosity than the unsaturated zone.
    C) The pore spaces in the saturated zone are full of water; the pore spaces in the
        unsaturated zone are not full of water.
    D) The pore spaces in the saturated zone are not full of water; the pore spaces in the
        unsaturated zone are full of water.
    Ans: C   Page: 286

23. Which of the following has the highest permeability?
    A) gravel   B) sandstone   C) shale   D) silt
    Ans: A   Page: 285

24. Which of the following statements about the water table is true?
    A) The water table changes when discharge is balanced by recharge.
    B) The water table has the same general shape as the topography.
    C) The water table is well below the land surface beneath lakes.
    D) The water table is elevated near high volume pumping wells.
    Ans: B   Page: 286

25. Which of the following statements is true?
    A) Influent streams discharge groundwater and are characteristic of arid regions.
    B) Influent streams discharge groundwater and are characteristic of humid regions.
    C) Influent streams recharge groundwater and are characteristic of arid regions.
    D) Influent streams recharge groundwater and are characteristic of humid regions.
    Ans: C   Page: 286

26. Which of the following represents the boundary between the saturated zone and the unsaturated zone?
    A) aquifer   B) aquiclude   C) groundwater table   D) porosity
    Ans: C   Page: 286

27. Which of the following statements regarding effluent streams is true?
    A) Effluent streams recharge groundwater and are characteristic of humid regions.
    B) Effluent streams recharge groundwater and are characteristic of arid regions.
    C) Effluent streams are fed by groundwater and are characteristic of humid regions.
    D) Effluent streams are fed by groundwater and are characteristic of arid regions.
    Ans: C   Page: 286

Use the following to answer questions 28-30:

The following questions refer to the cross section below:

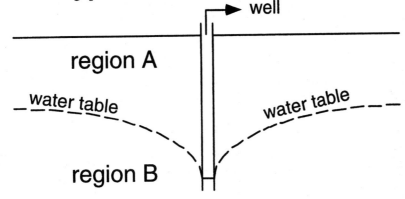

28. Region A is the _____.
    A) discharge zone   B) recharge zone   C) saturated zone   D) unsaturated zone
    Ans: D   Page: 286

29. Region B is the _____.
    A) discharge zone   B) recharge zone   C) saturated zone   D) unsaturated zone
    Ans: C   Page: 286

30. The lowering of the water table near the well is called a(n) _____.
    A) aquiclude   B) cone of depression   C) influent zone   D) sinkhole
    Ans: B   Page: 288

Use the following to answer question 31:

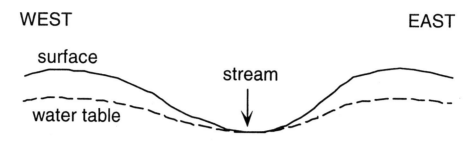

WEST   EAST

surface   stream

water table

31. Based on the geometry of the surface and water table depicted in the cross section above, which of the following statements is true?
A) The stream is gaining water from the groundwater.
B) The stream is losing water to the groundwater.
C) The stream is gaining water from the groundwater on the west side and losing water to the groundwater on the east side.
D) The stream and the groundwater are not connected.
Ans: A   Page: 286-287

32. What type of aquifer is bounded above and below by relatively impermeable beds?
A) aquiclude   B) confined   C) perched   D) unconfined
Ans: B   Alternative Location: Online quizzing   Page: 286

33. If the amount of discharge in an aquifer exceeds the amount of recharge, the groundwater table _____.
A) will rise
B) will drop
C) will remain the same
D) may rise or drop depending on the permeability
Ans: B   Page: 286-288

34. Which of the following is not caused by overpumping groundwater?
A) intrusion of salt water into coastal aquifers
B) depletion of an aquifer
C) raising of the land surface
D) development of cracks and fissures at the surface
Ans: C   Page: 288-290

35. Which of the following statements about groundwater is <u>true</u>?
    A) At the coast, salty groundwater lies on top of fresh groundwater.
    B) Groundwater moves from areas where the water table is low to areas where the water table is high.
    C) The higher the permeability of an aquifer, the faster the groundwater will flow.
    D) The steeper the water-table slope, the slower the groundwater will flow.
    Ans: C   Page: 290

36. Darcy's Law states that the volume of water flowing through a cross-sectional area per time is equal to _____.
    A) porosity × hydraulic conductivity
    B) porosity × water table slope
    C) hydraulic conductivity × water table slope
    D) porosity × hydraulic conductivity × water table slope
    Ans: C   Page: 290-292

37. According to Darcy's Law, which of the following aquifers will have the greatest rate of groundwater flow?
    A) an aquifer with high hydraulic conductivity and a high hydraulic gradient
    B) an aquifer with high hydraulic conductivity and a low hydraulic gradient
    C) an aquifer with low hydraulic conductivity and a high hydraulic gradient
    D) an aquifer with low hydraulic conductivity and a low hydraulic gradient
    Ans: A   Page: 290-292

38. Which of the following statements about groundwater in coastal regions is <u>true</u>?
    A) Fresh water is denser than seawater, therefore fresh groundwater floats on top of salty groundwater.
    B) Fresh water is denser than seawater, therefore salty groundwater floats on top of fresh groundwater.
    C) Seawater is denser than fresh water, therefore fresh groundwater floats on top of salty groundwater.
    D) Seawater is denser than fresh water, therefore salty groundwater floats on top of fresh groundwater.
    Ans: C   Page: 290

39. How fast does most groundwater move in aquifers?
    A) a few centimeters per day   C) a few kilometers per day
    B) a few meters per day   D) a few tens of kilometers per day
    Ans: A   Page: 292

40. In what type of rock do most caves form?
    A) granite   B) limestone   C) sandstone   D) shale
    Ans: B   Page: 292

41. The Ogallala aquifer in the southwestern high plains of Texas and New Mexico consists of _____.
    A) basalt and gabbro   C) sand and gravel
    B) limestone and dolostone   D) shale and mudstone
    Ans: C   Page: 293

42. Karst topography forms in regions underlain by _____.
    A) basalt   B) limestone   C) sandstone   D) shale
    Ans: B   Page: 294

43. Stalagmites _____.
    A) form in sandstone fractures   C) grow up from the floor of a cave
    B) form in the pore spaces of a limestone   D) hang down from the ceiling of a cave
    Ans: C   Page: 294

44. Sinkholes are a possible danger in regions underlain by what type of bedrock?
    A) granite   B) limestone   C) sandstone   D) shale
    Ans: B   Page: 294

45. Which of the following statements about karst topography is false?
    A) Karst topography contains sinkholes.
    B) Karst topography forms from freezing and thawing of groundwater.
    C) Karst topography does not have a normal river drainage system.
    D) Karst topography forms in regions where subsurface limestone is dissolved by groundwater.
    Ans: B   Page: 294

46. Which of the following characteristics favors the development of karst topography?
    A) high rainfall and fractured limestone bedrock
    B) high rainfall and fractured sandstone bedrock
    C) low rainfall and fractured limestone bedrock
    D) low rainfall and fractured sandstone bedrock
    Ans: A   Page: 294

47. Trichlorethylene (TCE), a serious groundwater contaminant, is used in _____.
    A) agriculture   C) wastewater treatment systems
    B) industrial processes   D) all of the above
    Ans: B   Page: 295

48. Groundwater in agricultural areas may contain high quantities of _____ due to fertilizers.
    A) calcium   B) lead   C) nitrate   D) sodium
    Ans: C   Page: 295

49. As one goes deeper in the Earth's crust, _____.
    A) the porosity increases and the concentration of dissolved minerals increases
    B) the porosity increases and the concentration of dissolved minerals decreases
    C) the porosity decreases and the concentration of dissolved minerals increases
    D) the porosity decreases and the concentration of dissolved minerals decreases
    Ans: C   Page: 297

50. Most of the water coming out of continental hot springs is _____.
    A) magmatic water   B) metamorphic water   C) meteoric water   D) seawater
    Ans: C   Page: 298

Chapter 14: Rivers: Transport to the Oceans

1. Which of the following is the most important erosional force?
   A) glaciers   B) streams   C) waves   D) wind
   Ans: B   Page: 303

2. Because of human activity, sediment transport by streams has _____.
   A) decreased by 100%   C) increased by 10%
   B) decreased by 10%   D) increased by 100%
   Ans: D   Page: 303

3. Which of the following is a measure of a fluid's resistance to flow?
   A) capacity   B) competence   C) permeability   D) viscosity
   Ans: D   Page: 304

4. Which of the following sets of conditions would favor turbulent flow as opposed to laminar flow?
   A) high fluid viscosity and high flow velocity
   B) high fluid viscosity and low flow velocity
   C) low fluid viscosity and high flow velocity
   D) low fluid viscosity and low flow velocity
   Ans: C   Page: 304-305

5. Which of the following flows is most likely to be turbulent?
   A) slow flow in a shallow channel   C) slow flow in a deep channel
   B) fast flow in a shallow channel   D) fast flow in a deep channel
   Ans: D   Page: 304-305

6. Which of the following statements about fluid flow is <u>false</u>?
   A) As the velocity of a stream increases, laminar flow may change to turbulent flow.
   B) The viscosity of most fluids increases as temperature increases.
   C) Most streams and rivers are turbulent.
   D) The more viscous the fluid, the more likely the flow is laminar.
   Ans: B   Page: 305

7. Which of the following terms describes the total sediment load carried by a stream?
   A) capacity   B) competence   C) discharge   D) viscosity
   Ans: A   Page: 305

8. Which of the following statements about streams is <u>false</u>?
   A) Faster currents can carry larger particles than slower currents.
   B) Laminar flows generally carry more sediment than turbulent flows.
   C) Smaller particles settle more slowly than larger particles.
   D) The base level is the lowest level to which a stream can erode.
   Ans: B   Page: 305

9. Suspended load includes all material _____.
   A) rolling along the bottom of the stream
   B) temporarily or permanently suspended in the flow
   C) deposited on the bottom of the stream
   D) rolling along the bottom <u>and</u> suspended in the flow
   Ans: B   Page: 305

10. Which of the following is considered part of a stream's bed load?
    A) dissolved salts   C) saltating sand grains
    B) gravel sliding along the bottom   D) suspended clay particles
    Ans: B   Page: 305

11. As the velocity of a stream current increases, _____ .
    A) more of the bed material is in motion
    B) progressively finer particles are suspended
    C) the suspended load decreases
    D) total capacity decreases
    Ans: A   Page: 305

12. Sand grains will <u>not</u> be transported by a stream unless the stream velocity exceeds
    _____.
    A) 2 centimeters per second   C) 2 meters per second
    B) 20 centimeters per second   D) 20 meters per second
    Ans: B   Page: 306

13. During turbulent flow, smaller grains will <u>not</u> _____.
    A) be picked up more frequently than large grains
    B) jump higher than large grains
    C) settle more quickly than large grains
    D) travel farther than large grains
    Ans: C   Page: 306

14. Which of the following particles is the most easily eroded from the bed of a stream?
    A) boulders   B) cohesive clay   C) pebbles   D) sand
    Ans: D   Page: 306

15. Which of the following materials is <u>most</u> likely to be transported as suspended load?
    A) boulders   B) clay   C) gravel   D) sand
    Ans: B   Page: 306

16. The long dimension of a ripple forms _____ to the current direction.
    A) parallel   B) at a 45° angle   C) at a 60° angle   D) perpendicular
    Ans: D   Page: 306

17. In a sand dune in a river, _____ occurs on the upstream side of the dune and _____ occurs on the downstream side of the dune.
    A) deposition. . . deposition   C) erosion . . . deposition
    B) deposition . . . erosion   D) erosion . . . erosion
    Ans: C   Page: 306

18. Which of the following correctly lists the order of bed forms which develop with increasing current velocity?
    A) dunes → ripples → flat beds   C) ripples → dunes → flat beds
    B) flat beds → dunes → ripples   D) ripples → flat beds → dunes
    Ans: C   Page: 307

19. Which of the following terms describes a curved, coarse-grained deposit that forms on the inside curve of a stream?
    A) dune   B) meander   C) oxbow   D) point bar
    Ans: D   Page: 309

20. Curves and bends in a stream channel are called _____.
    A) alluvial fans   B) braids   C) deltas   D) meanders
    Ans: D   Page: 309

21. At a bend in a river, _____ occurs on the outside of the bend and _____ occurs on the inside of the bend.
    A) deposition. . . deposition   C) erosion . . . deposition
    B) deposition . . . erosion   D) erosion . . . erosion
    Ans: C   Page: 309-310

Use the following to answer question 22:

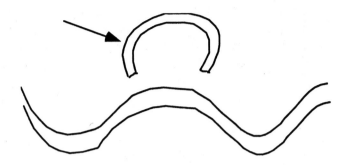

22. In the map of a stream above, the arrow is pointing to a(n) _____.
   A) natural levee   B) oxbow lake   C) point bar   D) sand dune
   Ans: B   Page: 310-311

23. Oxbow lakes are associated with which of the following types of rivers?
   A) braided rivers   B) dendritic rivers   C) meandering rivers   D) straight rivers
   Ans: C   Page: 311

24. In which of the following locations would one most likely find a braided stream?
   A) at the edge of a melting glacier
   B) on a gently sloping plain of fine-grained sediment
   C) in a narrow gorge cut into bedrock
   D) all of the above
   Ans: A   Page: 310-311

25. The volume of water flowing past a given point in a given time is called the _____.
   A) capacity   B) competence   C) discharge   D) viscosity
   Ans: C   Page: 312

26. Which of the following would be the most fertile area for crops?
   A) a stream channel   C) a natural levee
   B) a floodplain   D) an uplands area away from the stream
   Ans: B   Page: 312

27. Which of the following discharge equations is correct?
   A) $\text{discharge} = \dfrac{\text{width}}{(\text{depth} \times \text{velocity})}$ C) discharge = width × depth × velocity

   B) $\text{discharge} = \dfrac{(\text{width} \times \text{depth})}{\text{velocity}}$ D) $\text{discharge} = \dfrac{(\text{width} \times \text{velocity})}{\text{depth}}$

   Ans: C   Page: 312

28. Which of the following depositional settings consists primarily of fine-grained silt and mud?
    A) stream channels   B) floodplains   C) natural levees   D) point bars
    Ans: B   Page: 311-312

29. What are the dimensions (units) of stream discharge?
    A) cubic meters   C) square meters per second
    B) meters per second   D) cubic meters per second
    Ans: D   Page: 312

30. For most rivers, discharge _____ downstream.
    A) increases   B) remains constant   C) decreases slightly   D) decreases greatly
    Ans: A   Page: 312

31. For a given river, which of the following floods would have the largest discharge?
    A) a 5-year flood
    B) a 20-year flood
    C) a 100-year flood
    D) one cannot tell from the information provided
    Ans: C   Page: 314

32. Which of the following statements regarding floods is true?
    A) A 50-year flood has a 2% chance of occurring in any one year.
    B) A 50-year flood is generally larger than a 100-year flood.
    C) A 50-year flood occurs more frequently than a 5-year flood.
    D) A 50-year flood on one river is the same size as a 50-year flood on another river.
    Ans: A   Alternative Location: Online quizzing   Page: 314

33. At any point in a river, the equilibrium between erosion of the streambed and sedimentation in the channel is controlled by _____.
    A) climate   B) stream flow   C) topography   D) all of the above
    Ans: D   Page: 315

34. Which of the following describes the shape of the longitudinal profile of a stream?
    A) a concave downward curve   C) a horizontal line
    B) a concave upward curve   D) a straight line sloping downstream
    Ans: B   Page: 315

35. Which of the following statements regarding graded streams is true?
    A) Coarse-grained sediments accumulate at the mouth of the stream; finer-grained sediments are deposited at the head of the stream.
    B) The discharge is constant from the head of the stream to the mouth.
    C) The slope of the stream is constant from head to mouth.
    D) There is a balance between erosion and sedimentation.
    Ans: D   Page: 316

36. If a dam is built, sediment will _____ on the upstream side of the dam and sediment will _____ on the downstream side of the dam.
    A) accumulate . . . accumulate
    B) accumulate . . . erode
    C) erode . . . accumulate
    D) erode . . . erode
    Ans: B   Page: 316-317

37. What is the primary reason sediment is deposited in large cone-shaped deposits at mountain fronts?
    A) because stream valleys widen abruptly at a mountain front
    B) because stream valleys narrow abruptly at a mountain front
    C) because stream valleys get much steeper at a mountain front
    D) because stream valleys get less steep at a mountain front
    Ans: A   Page: 317

38. Large, cone-shaped deposits of sediment at a mountain front are called _____.
    A) alluvial fans   B) deltas   C) natural levees   D) terraces
    Ans: A   Page: 317

39. In an alluvial fan, the coarsest material would be deposited _____.
    A) on the steep, upper slopes of the fan
    B) on the gentle, lower slopes of the fan
    C) approximately halfway between the steep slopes of the mountains and the gentle slopes of the plains
    D) where two fans interfere or overlap one another
    Ans: A   Page: 317

40. Which of the following statements regarding stream terraces is <u>true</u>?
    A) Terraces are composed of bedrock and form as a result of rapid subsidence.
    B) Terraces are composed of bedrock and form as a result of rapid uplift.
    C) Terraces are composed of floodplain deposits and form as a result of rapid subsidence.
    D) Terraces are composed of floodplain deposits and form as a result of rapid uplift.
    Ans: D   Page: 317

41. Which of the following lakes is the world's largest and deepest?
    A) Great Salt Lake, North America
    B) Lake Baikal, Asia
    C) Lake Superior, North America
    D) Lake Victoria, Africa
    Ans: B   Page: 318

42. In North America, the continental divide that separates water that flows into the Atlantic Ocean from water that flows into the Pacific Ocean is located _____.
    A) in the Sierra Nevada, California
    B) in the Appalachian Mountains
    C) in the Rocky Mountains
    D) along the Mississippi River
    Ans: C   Page: 319

Use the following to answer question 43:

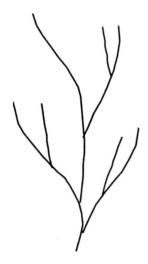

43. What type of drainage pattern is depicted in the map above?
    A) dendritic   B) radial   C) rectangular   D) trellis
    Ans: A   Page: 319

44. What type of drainage network would you expect to find on a volcano?
    A) dendritic drainage   C) rectangular drainage
    B) radial drainage   D) trellis drainage
    Ans: B   Page: 319

45. How far can large rivers, such as the Amazon, maintain a current out to sea?
    A) meters   B) 10s of meters   C) 100s of meters   D) many kilometers
    Ans: D   Page: 321

46. Where do deltas form?
    A) at drainage divides   C) at mountain fronts
    B) at meander loops   D) at river mouths
    Ans: D   Page: 321

47. Which of the following beds in a delta consists of the coarsest sediment?
    A) bottomset beds
    B) foreset beds
    C) topset beds
    D) All of the above contain similar amounts of coarse sediment.
    Ans: C   Page: 321

48. On a delta, smaller rivers that branch off downstream are called _____.
    A) distributaries   B) divides   C) rivulets   D) tributaries
    Ans: A   Page: 321

49. Which of the following best explains why there are no large deltas on the east coast of North America?
    A) because no rivers empty out along the east coast of North America
    B) because the Appalachian Mountains are too resistant to erosion
    C) because the rivers of the east coast have currents that are too weak to carry much sediment
    D) because the waves and tides in the Atlantic Ocean are too strong
    Ans: D   Page: 322

50. Why is the Mississippi delta so large?
    A) because the Mississippi River transports a huge amount of sediment
    B) because tides in the Gulf of Mexico are not very strong
    C) because waves in the Gulf of Mexico are not very strong
    D) all of the above
    Ans: D   Page: 321-322

Chapter 15: Winds and Deserts

1. Eolian processes are powered by _____.
   A) glaciers   B) ocean currents   C) streams   D) wind
   Ans: D   Page: 327

2. Which of the following statements is <u>true</u>?
   A) Air flows and stream flows are mostly laminar.
   B) Air flows are mostly laminar; stream flows are mostly turbulent.
   C) Air flows are mostly turbulent; stream flows are mostly laminar.
   D) Air flows and stream flows are mostly turbulent.
   Ans: D   Page: 328

3. For the same velocity, why is air flow more turbulent than water flow?
   A) because air has a lower density than water
   B) because air has a lower viscosity than water
   C) because air is less confined by solid boundaries than water
   D) <u>all</u> of the above
   Ans: D   Page: 328

4. From what direction do the trade winds in the tropics blow?
   A) east   B) north   C) south   D) west
   Ans: A   Page: 328

5. In the temperate zones of the Earth between 30° and 60° latitude, the prevailing winds come from the _____.
   A) east   B) north   C) south   D) west
   Ans: D   Page: 328

Use the following to answer question 6:

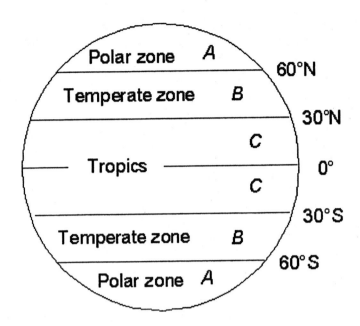

6. In the map of Earth above, where do the trade winds occur?
   A) in the regions labeled A
   B) in the regions labeled B
   C) in the regions labeled C
   D) in the regions labeled A, B, and C
   Ans: C   Page: 328

7. Due to the Coriolis effect, any large-scale current of air or water is deflected to the
   _____ in the northern hemisphere and to the _____ in the southern hemisphere.
   A) left . . . left   B) left . . . right   C) right . . . left   D) right . . . right
   Ans: C   Page: 328

8. Which of the following is an important source of dust?
   A) volcanic dust from eruptions
   B) clay minerals from soils
   C) organic sources, such as charcoal, pollen, and bacteria
   D) all of the above
   Ans: D   Page: 329

9. Why are streams able to move larger particles than wind?
   A) Air has a lower density and viscosity than water.
   B) Air does not obey the same laws of motion as water.
   C) Air moves at lower velocities than water.
   D) Air impedes the bounding movements of saltation.
   Ans: A   Page: 329

10. The amount of windblown material that a wind can carry does <u>not</u> depend upon the
    _____.
    A) particle size   B) surface material   C) temperature   D) wind strength
    Ans: C   Page: 329

11. For how long did fine-grained dust particles from the eruption of Mt. Pinatubo remain in
    the atmosphere?
    A) several days   B) several weeks   C) several months   D) several years
    Ans: D   Page: 330

12. Which of the following processes does not increase the amount of dust in the
    atmosphere?
    A) agriculture   B) deforestation   C) erosion   D) precipitation
    Ans: D   Page: 330

13. Most windblown sand consists of _____.
    A) calcite   B) feldspar   C) gypsum   D) quartz
    Ans: D   Page: 330

14. Why does volcanic dust tend to travel farther than wind-blown dust derived from the
    continents?
    A) because volcanic dust is erupted high into the atmosphere
    B) because volcanic dust is less dense than dust derived from the continents
    C) because volcanic dust is composed of quartz, whereas dust derived from the
        continents is composed of feldspar
    D) <u>all</u> of the above
    Ans: A   Page: 330

15. Which of the following retards deflation?
    A) construction   B) motor vehicles   C) plowing   D) vegetation
    Ans: D   Page: 332

16. How do ventifacts form?
    A) by dissolution by dew
    B) by breaking apart of rocks along cracks
    C) by sandblasting
    D) by slow chemical weathering
    Ans: C   Page: 332

17. What type of environment yields quartz sand grains that are rounded and frosted?
    A) an eolian environment   C) an oceanic environment
    B) a glacial environment   D) a stream environment
    Ans: A   Page: 332

18. What is the primary cause of frosting present in the surface of quartz sand grains in the desert?
    A) abrasion by air currents
    C) dissolution by dew
    B) chemical reaction with feldspar grains
    D) impacts with other sand grains
    Ans: C   Page: 332

19. How does desert pavement form?
    A) by intense chemical weathering
    C) by stream erosion
    B) by intense mechanical weathering
    D) by wind erosion
    Ans: D   Page: 332-333

20. Which of the following is a coarse, gravelly ground surface that results from the removal of fine-grained particles by wind erosion?
    A) alluvial fan   B) desert pavement   C) pediment   D) talus slope
    Ans: B   Page: 332-333

21. Which of the following processes describes the gradual erosion of the ground surface by wind?
    A) deflation   B) desertification   C) solifluction   D) subsidence
    Ans: A   Page: 332

22. Why do sand grains saltating in air "jump" higher than sand grains saltating in water?
    A) because air flow is more laminar than water flow
    B) because air is denser than water
    C) because air is less viscous than water
    D) because air is warmer than water
    Ans: C   Page: 334-335

23. The cross beds exposed in an eolian sandstone dip to the west. During the deposition of the sand, the prevailing winds were probably from the _____.
    A) east   B) north   C) south   D) west
    Ans: A   Page: 335

24. Sand will accumulate _____ of a boulder.
    A) mostly on the leeside (downwind)
    B) mostly on the windward side (upwind)
    C) equally on the leeside and the windward side
    D) neither on the leeside nor on the windward side
    Ans: A   Page: 335

Use the following to answer question 25:

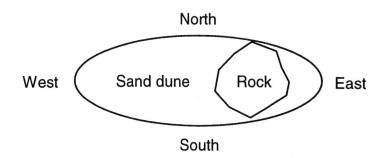

North

West   Sand dune   Rock   East

South

25. Given the relative positions of the sand dune and rock shown above, the wind direction is predominantly _____.
A) north to south   B) south to north   C) east to west   D) west to east
Ans: C   Page: 335

26. What type of sedimentary deposit results from the settling of fine-grained particles from a dust cloud?
A) loess   B) playa   C) pediment   D) sand dune
Ans: A   Page: 336

27. During erosion, loess tends to break off _____.
A) in horizontal layers   C) along irregular cracks
B) in vertical sheets   D) slowly, grain-by-grain
Ans: B   Page: 336-337

28. The loess deposited in the Upper Mississippi Valley was derived primarily from _____.
A) coastal sand dunes   C) glacial deposits
B) desert regions lying to the west   D) volcanic dust
Ans: C   Page: 336, 338

Use the following to answer questions 29-30:

The following questions refer to the map view of a sand dune.

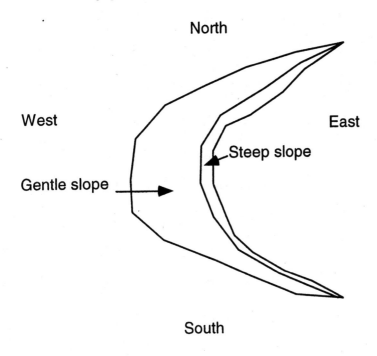

29. The sand dune shown above is a _____ dune.
    A) barchan   B) blowout   C) linear   D) transverse
    Ans: A   Page: 337

30. Which direction does the prevailing wind blow in the diagram above?
    A) north to south   B) south to north   C) east to west   D) west to east
    Ans: D   Page: 337

31. Which of the following is a crescent-shaped dune?
    A) barchan   B) loess   C) pediment   D) transverse
    Ans: A   Page: 337

32. Long wavy sand ridges that lie perpendicular to the prevailing wind are called _____.
    A) barchan dunes   B) blowout dunes   C) linear dunes   D) transverse dunes
    Ans: D   Page: 337

33. Sand dunes behind beaches are typically _____.
    A) barchan dunes   B) blowout dunes   C) linear dunes   D) transverse dunes
    Ans: D   Page: 337

34. Long sand ridges that are more or less parallel to the prevailing wind are called _____.
    A) barchan dunes   B) blowout dunes   C) linear dunes   D) transverse dunes
    Ans: C   Page: 337

35. How much of Earth's land area is covered by arid regions?
    A) 5%   B) 20%   C) 50%   D) 80%
    Ans: B   Page: 338

36. Which of the following best explains why the Sahara desert of Africa exists?
    A) The Sahara desert lies in the rain shadow of coastal mountains.
    B) The Sahara desert lies near 30°N latitude.
    C) The Sahara desert lies thousands of kilometers from the ocean.
    D) The sandy soil of the Sahara desert drains so quickly that vegetation is unable to
        grow.
    Ans: B   Page: 338

37. Which of the following statements is <u>false</u>?
    A) Deserts form under virtually stationary areas of low atmospheric pressure.
    B) Deserts form far inland where air has already lost its moisture through precipitation.
    C) Deserts form where air is so cold only small amounts of moisture can precipitate.
    D) Deserts form where moisture-bearing winds are blocked by mountain ranges.
    Ans: A   Page: 338

38. Which of the following best explains why the Great Basin and Mojave deserts of
    western North America exist?
    A) The two deserts lie in the rain shadow of coastal mountains.
    B) The two deserts lie in the trade winds.
    C) The two deserts lie near the equator.
    D) The two deserts lie thousands of kilometers from the ocean.
    Ans: A   Page: 338

39. Over the past 20 million years, the interior of Australia has changed from a moist,
    humid climate to a desert. Why?
    A) because plate collisions have built mountains near the coastline that block moisture-
        bearing winds from the continent's interior
    B) because Australia has moved northward into an arid, subtropical zone
    C) because Australia has moved southward out of the path of the more humid trade
        winds
    D) because the continent has grown through volcanic activity, making the interior too
        far away from moisture-bearing winds
    Ans: B   Page: 339

40. Which of the following is <u>not</u> a cause of desertification?
    A) cattle grazing
    B) climate change
    C) irrigation
    D) latitude changes caused by plate tectonics
    Ans: C   Page: 339

41. Radar imaging from the space shuttle Endeavor has provided evidence that the Sahara
    Desert _____.
    A) has always been an arid environment
    B) was once a tropical region, with many different types of vegetation
    C) once had an extensive system of river channels, which are now dry
    D) has sand dunes in excess of 300 m in height
    Ans: C   Page: 339

42. Much of a desert's surface consists of sand, gravel, and rock rubble because

    _____.
    A) clay minerals form slowly in a desert environment
    B) wind blows away clay and soil before it can accumulate to great thickness
    C) vegetation is sparse and cannot prevent erosion of soil
    D) <u>all</u> of the above
    Ans: D   Page: 339-340

43. Desert varnish is composed of all of the following <u>except</u> _____.
    A) carbonate minerals   B) clay minerals   C) iron oxides   D) manganese oxides
    Ans: A   Page: 340

44. What causes most of the erosion in deserts?
    A) groundwater   B) streams   C) thermal cycling   D) wind
    Ans: B   Page: 340

45. What minerals are responsible for the orange-brown colors of weathered surfaces in the
    desert?
    A) carbonates   B) framework silicates   C) iron oxides   D) sulfates
    Ans: C   Page: 340

46. Which of the following best describes the deposit left by a flash flood?
    A) a combination of desert pavement and loess
    B) a flat deposit of coarse debris
    C) channel, levee, and floodplain deposits
    D) thin deposits of evaporites
    Ans: B   Page: 340

47. How much of the Sahara desert is covered with sand and sand dunes?
    A) approximately 1%   C) approximately 50%
    B) approximately 10%   D) approximately 90%
    Ans: B   Page: 341

48. Temporary lakes that accumulate in arid desert basins are called _____ lakes.
    A) eolian   B) erg   C) playa   D) wadi
    Ans: C   Page: 341

49. Small desert valleys are called wadis in the Middle East and _____ in the western United States.
    A) dry washes   B) ergs   C) loess   D) pediments
    Ans: A   Alternative Location: Online quizzing   Page: 343

50. Which of the following is a broad, gently sloping platform of bedrock that is left behind as a mountain front eroded in the desert?
    A) alluvial fan   B) erg   C) mesa   D) pediment
    Ans: D   Page: 343

Chapter 16: The Work of Ice

1. How much of the land surface is covered by ice?
   A) approximately 10%
   B) approximately 30%
   C) approximately 50%
   D) approximately 80%
   Ans: A   Page: 347

2. Which of the following is an extremely slow-moving sheet of ice that covers vast land areas?
   A) an arete   B) a continental glacier   C) an ice shelf   D) a valley glacier
   Ans: B   Page: 349

3. How thick are the Greenland and Antarctic ice caps?
   A) approximately 100 meters thick
   B) approximately 300 meters thick
   C) approximately 1 kilometer thick
   D) approximately 3 kilometers thick
   Ans: D   Page: 350

4. Where is the largest mass of ice on Earth located?
   A) Antarctica   B) Greenland   C) Himalayas   D) Siberia
   Ans: A   Page: 350

5. Why are the Earth's poles colder than the equator?
   A) because the Earth's poles are farther from the Sun than the Earth's equator
   B) because the sun strikes the Earth at a lower angle at the poles than at the equator
   C) because there are fewer hours of sunlight at the poles than at the equator
   D) because there is more snow at the poles than at the equator
   Ans: B   Page: 350

6. The snow line is _____.
   A) the lowest altitude at which snow will fall in summer
   B) the lowest altitude at which snow will fall in winter
   C) the altitude above which snow does not completely melt in summer
   D) the altitude above which snow does not completely melt in winter
   Ans: C   Page: 350

7. At the equator, at what altitude does the snow line lie?
   A) less than 1000 meters
   B) about 2500 meters
   C) about 5000 meters
   D) about 10,000 meters
   Ans: C   Page: 352

8. Which of the following lists is written in order of <u>increasing</u> ice "metamorphism"?
   A) snow → granular ice → firn → glacial ice
   B) snow → firn → glacial ice → granular ice
   C) snow → firn → granular ice → glacial ice
   D) snow → granular ice → glacial ice → firn
   Ans: A   Page: 352

9. A snow deposit contains approximately 90% air. How much air does glacial ice contain?
   A) approximately 5%   C) approximately 50%
   B) approximately 20%   D) approximately 90%
   Ans: B   Page: 352

10. Which of the following forms of ice has the greatest density?
    A) firn   B) glacial ice   C) granular ice   D) snow
    Ans: B   Page: 352

11. Which of the following describes the transformation of ice to gaseous water vapor?
    A) boiling   B) calving   C) melting   D) sublimation
    Ans: D   Page: 352

12. If accumulation exceeds ablation, then _____.
    A) the glacial ice will flow downhill and the glacial front will move downhill
    B) the glacial ice will flow downhill, but the glacial front will move uphill
    C) the glacial ice will flow uphill, but the glacial front will move downhill
    D) the glacial ice will flow uphill and the glacial front will move uphill
    Ans: A   Page: 352

13. In a bitterly cold climate, glaciers will move primarily by _____.
    A) basal slip   B) calving   C) plastic flow   D) sublimation
    Ans: C   Page: 355

14. Lake Vostok is _____.
    A) a former alpine lake that is now frozen into a glacier.
    B) a lake that lies under the Antarctic ice cap.
    C) a lake that lies on top of the Antarctic ice cap.
    D) a very large kettle lake
    Ans: B   Page: 355

15. Which of the following statements is correct?
    A) Continental and valley glaciers both move mostly by basal slip.
    B) Continental and valley glaciers both move mostly by plastic flow.
    C) Continental glaciers move mostly by basal slip; valley glaciers move mostly by plastic flow.
    D) Continental glaciers move mostly by plastic flow; valley glaciers move mostly by basal slip.
    Ans: C   Page: 355

16. Why do glacial crevasses form?
    A) because glacial meltwater erodes small valleys as glacial rivers flow
    B) because plate tectonic forces deform the glacier
    C) because the glacial surface deforms brittlely and cracks as the ice flows
    D) because the glacial surface partially melts, leaving holes and cracks
    Ans: C   Page: 357

Use the following to answer question 17:

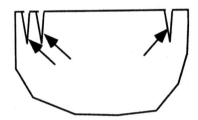

17. In the cross-section of a glacier above, the arrows point to _____.
    A) ablation surfaces   B) blocks of bedrock   C) crevasses   D) ice streams
    Ans: C   Page: 357

18. In a valley glacier, where is the ice velocity the fastest?
    A) along the base of the glacier
    B) along the sides of the glacier
    C) along the top center of the glacier
    D) None of the above. The ice velocity is constant throughout the glacier.
    Ans: C   Page: 357

19. How fast can surging glaciers move?
    A) about 5 meters per year   C) about 5 kilometers per year
    B) about 100 meters per year   D) about 100 kilometers per year
    Ans: C   Page: 357

20. Which of the following will cause sea level to rise?
    A) melting of a very large iceberg   C) melting of the Ross ice shelf
    B) melting of the Greenland ice cap   D) all of the above
    Ans: B   Page: 360-361

21. If a very large iceberg in the ocean were to melt, what would happen to sea level?
    A) Sea level would decrease slightly.
    B) Sea level would remain the same.
    C) Sea level would increase slightly.
    D) Sea level would decrease or increase depending on the air content of the iceberg.
    Ans: B   Page: 359-360

Use the following to answer question 22:

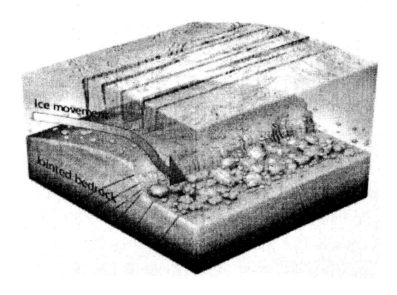

22. What glacial feature is depicted in the cross section above?
    A) drumlin   B) esker   C) kame   D) roche moutonée
    Ans: D   Page: 362

23. What are glacial striations?
    A) dust formed by grinding rocks to clay-sized particles during glacial movement
    B) grooves created by rocks scratching against bedrock at the base of a glacier
    C) large, streamlined hills of till and bedrock that parallel the direction of ice movement
    D) long, narrow, winding ridges of sand and gravel found in the middle of ground moraines
    Ans: B   Page: 362

24. Which of the following features can be used to determine the direction a continental glacier moved?
    A) drumlins   B) roches moutonées   C) striations   D) all of the above
    Ans: D   Page: 362-365

25. When two cirques at the heads of adjacent valleys meet at the moutaintop, they produce a sharp, jagged crest called _____.
A) an arete   B) a drumlin   C) a fjord   D) a moraine
Ans: A   Page: 362-363

26. Which of the following erosional features is characteristic of rivers and <u>not</u> glaciers?
A) arete   B) cirque   C) roche moutonée   D) V-shaped valley
Ans: D   Page: 364

27. Which of the following terms describes a glacial erosional feature as opposed to a glacial deposit?
A) erratic   B) fjord   C) outwash   D) till
Ans: B   Page: 364

28. Which of the following glacial deposits is the most poorly sorted?
A) an esker   B) a kame   C) a moraine   D) a varve
Ans: C   Page: 365

29. What are erratics?
A) conflicting dates of glaciation obtained by dating organic material found in glaciers
B) cross beds that do not match the overall outwash cross-bedding scheme
C) large boulders deposited randomly by glaciers
D) valleys with glacial striations that oppose the striations in adjacent valleys
Ans: C   Page: 364

30. Which of the following agents of erosion deposits the most poorly sorted sediment?
A) ice   B) ocean currents   C) streams   D) wind
Ans: A   Page: 364

31. What are fjords?
A) amphitheater-like hollows carved from mountains by glaciers
B) glacial valleys flooded with seawater
C) long, winding ridges of sediment found in the middle of ground moraines
D) steep-sided lakes located on glacial outwash plains
Ans: B   Page: 364

32. Glacial drift that has been modified, sorted, and distributed by meltwater streams is called _____.
A) moraine   B) outwash   C) rock flour   D) till
Ans: B   Page: 364

33. What is the general term for <u>all</u> sediment of glacial origin?
A) drift   B) moraine   C) outwash   D) till
Ans: A   Page: 364

34. Which of the following terms describes an accumulation of rocky, sandy, or clayey material deposited at the end of a glacier?
    A) dune   B) esker   C) loess   D) moraine
    Ans: D   Page: 365

35. Which of the following would be the most suitable site for a commercial sand and gravel pit?
    A) an arete   B) a drumlin   C) a kame   D) a varve
    Ans: C   Page: 365-366

36. Which of the following is deposited directly from ice?
    A) esker   B) kame   C) moraine   D) varve
    Ans: C   Page: 365

37. Which of the following statements about varves is true?
    A) Clay layers are deposited in summer and silt layers are deposited in winter.
    B) Silt layers are deposited in summer and clay layers are deposited in winter.
    C) Sand layers are deposited in summer and gravel layers are deposited in winter.
    D) Gravel layers are deposited in summer and sand layers are deposited in winter.
    Ans: B   Page: 366

38. Which of the following is a depositional feature rather than an erosional feature?
    A) arete   B) cirque   C) esker   D) hanging valley
    Ans: C   Page: 367

39. How do kettles form?
    A) by melting of large blocks of ice left by a glacier
    B) by melting permafrost
    C) by meltwater streams running through glacial tunnels
    D) by seasonal deposition of coarse and fine sediment
    Ans: A   Page: 366

40. How much of the Earth's land surface is permanently frozen?
    A) approximately 1%   C) approximately 10%
    B) approximately 5%   D) approximately 25%
    Ans: D   Page: 367

41. How thick is permafrost?
    A) up to 5 meters thick   C) up to 500 meters thick
    B) up to 50 meters thick   D) up to 5000 meters thick
    Ans: C   Page: 367

42. The age of the last glacial period is dated by carbon-14 dating of _____.
    A) logs in the glacial drift
    B) marine organisms contained in glacial ice
    C) plant leaves contained in the glacial drift
    D) wooly mammoths in glacial ice
    Ans: A   Page: 369

43. When did the most recent ice ages occur?
    A) Jurassic Period   B) Paleozoic Era   C) Pleistocene Epoch   D) Pliocene Epoch
    Ans: C   Page: 369

44. During the peak of the last ice age, sea level was _____ than sea level today.
    A) approximately 1 meter lower   C) approximately 100 meters lower
    B) approximately 10 meters lower   D) approximately 1000 meters lower
    Ans: C   Page: 369

45. When did the last ice age end?
    A) about 100 years ago   C) about 1 million years ago
    B) about 10,000 years ago   D) about 100 million years ago
    Ans: B   Page: 369

46. Which of the following is not one of the possible explanations for previous ice ages?
    A) changes in the large-scale oceanic circulation
    B) increases in the amount of carbon dioxide in the atmosphere
    C) large land masses (continents) positioned at the poles
    D) periodic changes in the Earth's eccentricity
    Ans: B   Page: 372

47. If all of the world's ice were to melt, sea level would _____.
    A) not change   C) rise about 60 meters
    B) rise about 4 meters   D) rise about 800 meters
    Ans: C   Page: 371

48. What is precession?
    A) the angle between the Earth's axis of rotation and the vertical to the orbital plane
    B) the changes in climate as the Earth warms and cools
    C) the degree of ellipticity of Earth's orbit
    D) the wobble of the Earth's axis of rotation
    Ans: D   Page: 372

49. Carbon dioxide in the atmosphere _____.
    A) is high during glacial periods and high during interglacial periods
    B) is high during glacial periods and low during interglacial periods
    C) is low during glacial periods and high during interglacial periods
    D) is low during glacial periods and low during interglacial periods
    Ans: C   Page: 372

50. At what time in Earth's history do some geologists speculate that the Earth was completely covered in ice?
    A) 1.8 to 0.01 million years ago (Pleistocene)
    B) 300 to 250 million years ago (Pennsylvanian–Permian)
    C) 750 to 600 million years ago (Late Proterozoic)
    D) 4.5 to 4.0 billion years ago (Hadean)
    Ans: C   Page: 375

Chapter 17: Earth Beneath the Oceans

1. Which of the following statements is <u>false</u>?
   A) Deep-sea sedimentation leaves a more continuous geologic record than continental sedimentation.
   B) The oceans lack folded and faulted mountains like those on continents.
   C) The oldest oceanic crust is much younger than the oldest continental crust.
   D) Weathering and erosion are more important in the oceans than on continents.
   Ans: D Page: 380

Use the following to answer questions 2-5:

The following questions refer to the schematic topographic profile of the Atlantic Ocean seafloor from New England to the mid-ocean ridge.

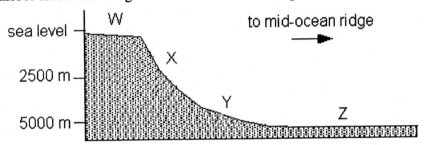

2. The area labeled "W" is the _____.
   A) abyssal plain B) continental rise C) continental shelf D) continental slope
   Ans: C Page: 384

3. The area labeled "X" is the _____.
   A) abyssal plain B) continental rise C) continental shelf D) continental slope
   Ans: D Page: 384

4. The area labeled "Y" is the _____.
   A) abyssal plain B) continental rise C) continental shelf D) continental slope
   Ans: B Page: 384

5. The area labeled "Z" is the _____.
   A) abyssal plain B) continental rise C) continental shelf D) continental slope
   Ans: A Page: 384

6. If one were to start from the east coast of North America and descend into the Atlantic Ocean, you would travel along the _____.
   A) continental rise then the continental shelf then the continental slope
   B) continental rise then the continental slope then the continental shelf
   C) continental shelf then the continental rise then the continental slope
   D) continental shelf then the continental slope then the continental rise
   Ans: D   Page: 384

7. Which of the following regions is a broad, flat, sand- and mud-covered platform that is part of the continent but slightly submerged?
   A) abyssal plain   B) continental rise   C) continental shelf   D) continental slope
   Ans: C   Page: 384

8. In which of the following locations would you most likely find outcrops of basalt on the ocean floor?
   A) on the abyssal plain
   B) on the continental rise
   C) on the continental shelf
   D) on the flank of a rift valley
   Ans: D   Page: 384

9. A traverse from North America across the Atlantic Ocean to continental Europe would reveal that the ocean floor _____.
   A) has high undersea mountains near both continents and is flat in the middle
   B) has deep trenches near both continents
   C) has a number of active volcanoes along most of the width of the traverse
   D) is approximately symmetric about the Mid-Atlantic Ridge
   Ans: D   Page: 384

10. Where is the ocean floor deepest?
    A) in oceanic trenches
    B) in rift valleys
    C) in submarine canyons
    D) on the abyssal plain
    Ans: B   Page: 385

11. How deep is the deepest part of the ocean?
    A) about 1 kilometer deep
    B) about 3 kilometers deep
    C) about 10 kilometers deep
    D) about 30 kilometers deep
    Ans: C   Page: 385

12. Graded beds of sand, silt, and mud deposited on submarine fans are called _____.
    A) alluvial fans   B) dunes   C) tills   D) turbidites
    Ans: D   Page: 389

13. Where does most volcanic activity on the seafloor take place?
    A) abyssal plains
    B) continental shelves
    C) mid-ocean ridges
    D) oceanic trenches
    Ans: C   Page: 386

14. Hydrothermal springs located on the floor of mid-ocean rift valleys can reach temperatures as high as approximately _____.
    A) 40 °C   B) 100 °C   C) 400 °C   D) 1000 °C
    Ans: C   Page: 386

15. Which of the following is an active continental margin?
    A) the east coast of Africa
    B) the east coast of North America
    C) the west coast of South America
    D) all of the above
    Ans: C   Page: 386

16. Which of the following are flat-topped seamounts, resulting from erosion of an island volcano when it was above sea level?
    A) guyots   B) mesas   C) pediments   D) stacks
    Ans: A   Page: 386

17. Which of the following statements is true?
    A) The continental shelf and continental slope are both shaped by turbidity currents.
    B) The continental shelf is shaped by turbidity currents, whereas the continental slope is shaped by waves.
    C) The continental shelf is shaped by waves, whereas the continental slope is shaped by turbidity currents.
    D) The continental shelf and continental slope are both shaped by waves.
    Ans: C   Page: 387-388

18. Which of the following currents erode and deposit fine-grained sediments on the continental slope and rise?
    A) longshore currents   B) river currents   C) tidal currents   D) turbidity currents
    Ans: D   Page: 388

19. Large fan-shaped deposits of fine-grained sediments that accumulate on the continental rise are called _____.
    A) alluvial fans   B) guyots   C) spits   D) submarine fans
    Ans: D   Page: 389

20. Which of the following materials would one expect to find on a continental shelf at a passive margin?
    A) basalt   B) pelagic sediments   C) terrigenous sediments   D) volcanic ash
    Ans: C   Page: 389

21. What are foraminifera shells, the most abundant biochemically precipitated pelagic sediment, made of?
    A) calcium carbonate   B) silicon dioxide   C) sodium chloride   D) iron sulfide
    Ans: A   Page: 389

22. Which of the following best describes pelagic sediments?
    A) deposited far from continental margins C) settle very slowly to the seafloor
    B) fine-grained   D) <u>all</u> of the above
    Ans: D   Page: 389

23. Pelagic sediments consist of all of the following <u>except</u>:
    A) calcareous oozes   B) quartz sands   C) silica oozes   D) terrigenous clays
    Ans: B   Page: 389-390

24. The shells of diatoms and radiolaria, which accumulate on the abyssal plain, are composed of _____.
    A) calcium carbonate   B) iron sulfide   C) silica   D) sodium chloride
    Ans: C   Page: 390

25. Which of the following statements about the deep ocean is <u>true</u>?
    A) Calcium carbonate is more soluble in the deep ocean than the shallow ocean.
    B) The deep ocean contains less carbon dioxide than the shallow ocean.
    C) The deep ocean is warmer than the shallow ocean.
    D) The pressure is lower in the deep ocean as compared to the shallow ocean.
    Ans: A   Page: 390

26. The height of an ocean wave increases as _____.
    A) the distance over which the wind blows over the water decreases
    B) the wind blows for longer times
    C) the wind speed decreases
    D) <u>all</u> of the above
    Ans: B   Page: 392

27. Waves cause small particles floating on the surface to move in _____.
    A) horizontal circular orbits   C) vertical circular orbits
    B) horizontal elliptical orbits   D) vertical elliptical orbits
    Ans: C   Page: 392-393

28. What creates ocean waves?
    A) gravitational forces   B) tectonic forces   C) solar forces   D) wind forces
    Ans: D   Page: 392

29. Why are there often irregular intervals between waves approaching the shore?
    A) because different storms in different locations produced the waves
    B) because the ocean temperatures vary
    C) because the underlying beach is irregular
    D) because the wind is often variable
    Ans: A   Page: 392

30. When a wave gets close to shore, water particles near the bottom move in _____ orbits.
    A) circular   B) elliptical   C) irregular   D) rectangular
    Ans: B   Page: 392

31. Which of the following equations correctly relates the velocity (*V*) of a wave to the wavelength (*L*) and period (*T*)?
    A) $V = L \times T$ B) $V = L / T$ C) $V = L^2 \times T$ D) $V = T / L$
    Ans: B   Page: 392

Use the following to answer questions 32-33:

The following questions refer to the wave cross section below.

32. In the diagram above, the wavelength is the distance _____.
    A) A-B   B) A-C   C) A-D   D) A-E
    Ans: B   Page: 393

33. In the diagram above, the distance F-H is called the _____.
    A) crest height   B) total displacement   C) trough height   D) wave height
    Ans: D   Page: 393

34. What causes the tides?
    A) earthquakes   B) gravity   C) ocean currents   D) wind
    Ans: B   Page: 394

35. As waves approach a beach, the rows of waves gradually bend to a direction more parallel to the shore. This change in direction is called _____.
    A) longshore drift   B) swash   C) tidal surge   D) wave refraction
    Ans: D   Page: 394

36. The zigzag motion that carries sand grains along a beach is known as _____.
    A) longshore drift   B) meandering   C) refraction   D) turbidity
    Ans: A   Page: 394

37. A rip current is a strong flow of water moving _____.
    A) parallel to the shore   C) at a 60° angle to the shore
    B) at a 30° angle to the shore   D) perpendicular to the shore
    Ans: D   Page: 394

38. Spring tides occur when _____.
    A) the Earth's centrifugal force is at a minimum
    B) the Earth is at a mid-point between its furthest point from the Sun and its closest point to the sun
    C) the Sun, Earth, and Moon are aligned in a straight line
    D) the Sun, Earth, and Moon form a right angle
    Ans: C   Page: 395

39. The extra-low tides that occur when the Sun, Earth, and Moon form a right angle are called _____ tides.
    A) autumn   B) neap   C) quarter   D) spring
    Ans: B   Page: 395

40. How many high tides are there in a day?
    A) 1   B) 2   C) 3   D) 4
    Ans: B   Page: 394

41. In Hawaii, the difference between low and high tides is approximately 0.5 m. In the Bay of Fundy in eastern Canada, the tidal range can reach _____.
    A) 1.2 m   B) 6 m   C) 12 m   D) 60 m
    Ans: C   Page: 395

42. What is the difference between tidal surges and tidal waves?
    A) Tidal surges are caused by the Moon; tidal waves are caused by the Sun.
    B) Tidal surges are caused by large storms; tidal waves are caused by undersea earthquakes.
    C) Tidal surges are larger than tidal waves.
    D) Tidal surges are made up of groups of tidal waves.
    Ans: B   Page: 396

43. What is a tsunami?
    A) a large wave caused by an undersea earthquake or landslide
    B) a strong current parallel to the coastline
    C) a tidal surge caused by a storm
    D) an unusually high tide that corresponds to the spring and fall equinoxes
    Ans: A   Page: 396

Use the following to answer questions 44-46:

The following questions refer to the beach profile below.

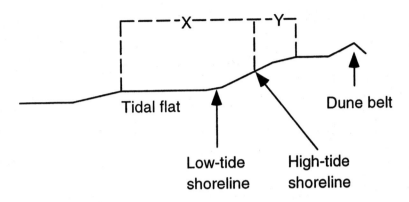

44. The area labeled "X" is called the _____.
    A) backshore   B) foreshore   C) surf zone   D) swash zone
    Ans: C   Page: 397

45. The area labeled "Y" is called the _____.
    A) backshore   B) foreshore   C) surf zone   D) swash zone
    Ans: D   Page: 397

46. Together, the areas labeled "X" and "Y" are called the _____.
    A) backshore   B) foreshore   C) surf zone   D) swash zone
    Ans: B   Page: 397

47. Which of the following terms describes isolated erosional remnants of rock left standing
    in the sea far from the shore?
    A) guyots   B) spits   C) stacks   D) wave-cut terraces
    Ans: C   Page: 398

48. Horizontal, planar, rocky surfaces that form in the surf zone as a result of wave erosion
    are called _____.
    A) backshores   B) barrier islands   C) stacks   D) wave-cut terraces
    Ans: D   Page: 398

49. Which of the following forms a barricade between the open ocean and the main
    shoreline?
    A) abyssal hills   B) barrier islands   C) guyots   D) wave-cut terraces
    Ans: B   Page: 399

50. How has sea level changed over the past century?
    A) Sea level has dropped 2 to5 m.
    B) Sea level has dropped 10 to 25 cm.
    C) Sea level has risen 10 to 25 cm.
    D) Sea level has risen 2 to 5 m.
    Ans: C   Page: 400

Chapter 18: Landscapes: Tectonic and Climate Interaction

1. Which of the following sciences is the study of landscapes and their evolution?
   A) geochronology   B) geology   C) geomorphology   D) topology
   Ans: C   Page: 407

2. On a topographic map, what type of lines connect points of equal elevation?
   A) contacts   B) contours   C) horizons   D) isograds
   Ans: B   Page: 408

3. On a topographic map, the more closely spaced the contour lines, _____.
   A) the higher the mountain
   B) the lower the mountain
   C) the gentler the slope
   D) the steeper the slope
   Ans: D   Page: 408

Use the following to answer questions 4-6:

The following questions refer to contour diagrams A, B, and C below. Note the different contour intervals.

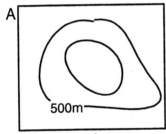

10 meters between contours

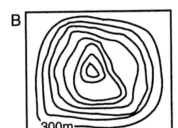

10 meters between contours

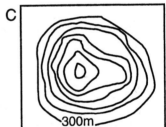

20 meters between contours

4. Which of the contour diagrams above depicts the landform with the highest elevation?
   A) diagram A
   B) diagram B
   C) diagram C
   D) cannot tell from information given
   Ans: A   Page: 408

5. Which of the contour diagrams above depicts the landform with the <u>lowest</u> relief?
   A) diagram A
   B) diagram B
   C) diagram C
   D) cannot tell from information given
   Ans: A   Page: 408

6. Which of the contour diagrams above depicts the landform with the <u>highest</u> relief?
   A) diagram A
   B) diagram B
   C) diagram C
   D) cannot tell from information given
   Ans: C   Page: 408

7. The vertical distance above sea level is called the _____.
   A) elevation   B) contour   C) relief   D) topography
   Ans: A   Page: 408

8. Which of the following best describes the relief of an area?
   A) the difference in elevation between the highest and lowest points
   B) the elevation of the highest point in the area relative to sea level
   C) the elevation of the lowest point in the area relative to sea level
   D) the steepest slope in the area measured in degrees
   Ans: A   Page: 409

9. On a global scale, the relief of the continental land surface is approximately _____.
   A) 3 kilometers   B) 9 kilometers   C) 30 kilometers   D) 90 kilometers
   Ans: B   Page: 410

10. Which of the following is written in order of <u>increasing</u> relief?
    A) Appalachian Mountains → Midwestern plains → Rocky Mountains
    B) Midwestern plains → Appalachian Mountains → Rocky Mountains
    C) Midwestern plains → Rocky Mountains → Appalachian Mountains
    D) Rocky Mountains → Appalachian Mountains → Midwestern plains
    Ans: B   Page: 410-411

11. Which of the following regions has the lowest elevation?
    A) Atlantic coast   B) Dead Sea   C) Death Valley   D) East African Rift
    Ans: B   Page: 410

12. The lowest continental land area in the world is located _____.
    A) at sea level
    B) 100 meters below sea level
    C) 400 meters below sea level
    D) 1000 meters below sea level
    Ans: C   Page: 410

13. What is the highest mountain in the world?
    A) Denali (Mt. McKinley)   B) Mt. Everest   C) Mt. Fuji   D) Mt. Shasta
    Ans: B   Page: 410

14. Which of the following regions has the lowest relief?
    A) the Appalachian Mountains
    B) the midwestern plains
    C) the Rocky Mountains
    D) <u>All</u> of the above have approximately the same relief.
    Ans: B   Page: 410-411

15. Which of the following regions in the United States has experienced the most recent tectonic uplift?
    A) central U.S.   B) northeastern U.S.   C) southeastern U.S.   D) western U.S.
    Ans: D   Page: 412

16. Landforms are the product of _____.
    A) erosion   B) sedimentation   C) tectonics   D) <u>all</u> of the above
    Ans: D   Page: 411

17. Which of the following geomorphic provinces lies between the Rocky Mountains and the Pacific Mountains?
    A) Appalachian highlands   C) Interior plain
    B) Interior highlands   D) Intermontane plateau
    Ans: D   Page: 411

18. Which of the following statements about mountains is <u>false</u>?
    A) The more recent the tectonic activity, the more likely the mountains are to be high.
    B) The steepest slopes are generally found in high mountains with great relief.
    C) Mountains are defined as landforms more than 1000 meters above sea level.
    D) The Himalayas have greater relief than the Appalachians.
    Ans: C   Page: 411

19. The characteristic landscapes resulting from erosion and sedimentation are called

    _____.
    A) bedding   B) contours   C) landforms   D) relief
    Ans: C   Page: 411

20. How high is Mount Everest, the highest mountain in the world?
    A) approximately 3000 meters   C) approximately 9000 meters
    B) approximately 6000 meters   D) approximately 12,000 meters
    Ans: C   Page: 410

21. The steepest slopes are generally found in _____.
    A) mountains with low elevations and low relief
    B) mountains with high elevations and low relief
    C) mountains with low elevations and high relief
    D) mountains with high elevations and high relief
    Ans: D   Page: 412

22. Which of the following is a small, flat-topped landform with steep slopes on all sides?
    A) cuesta   B) dome   C) mesa   D) plateau
    Ans: C   Page: 412

23. What is the average elevation of the Tibetan Plateau?
    A) 200 meters   B) 500 meters   C) 2000 meters   D) 5000 meters
    Ans: D   Page: 412

24. In a region that has been deformed into a series of anticlines and synclines, _____.
    A) anticlines always form ridges
    B) anticlines always form valleys
    C) anticlines form ridges during the early stages of landscape evolution, but may develop into valleys later
    D) anticlines form valleys during the early stages of landscape evolution, but may develop into ridges later
    Ans: C   Page: 413

25. The topography of the Valley and Ridge province in the Appalachian Mountains is controlled by _____.
    A) undeformed flat-lying sedimentary rocks
    B) sedimentary rocks deformed by anticlines and synclines
    C) sedimentary rocks cut by normal faults
    D) sedimentary rocks cut by reverse faults
    Ans: B   Page: 413

26. What is stream power?
    A) river slope plus river discharge   C) river slope times river discharge
    B) river slope minus river discharge   D) river slope divided by river discharge
    Ans: C   Page: 414

27. Which of the following processes is not a principal process by which bedrock is eroded?
    A) abrasion   B) current drag force   C) dissolution   D) glacial erosion
    Ans: C   Page: 416

28. The erosion of bedrock by suspended and saltating sediment is called _____.
    A) abrasion   B) diagenesis   C) dissolution   D) weathering
    Ans: A   Page: 416

29. Which of the following will increase the erosion of stream bedrock?
    A) decreasing the discharge   C) decreasing the stream slope
    B) decreasing the sediment grain size   D) increasing the sediment volume
    Ans: D   Page: 415

30. In which of the following stream valleys does the stream power exceed the resistance to erosion?
    A) a broad, flat lowland valley
    B) a steep V-shaped canyon
    C) a wide, open valley
    D) Stream power exceeds the resistance to erosion in <u>all</u> of the above.
    Ans: B   Page: 415

Use the following to answer question 31:

The following question refers to the geologic cross-section below:

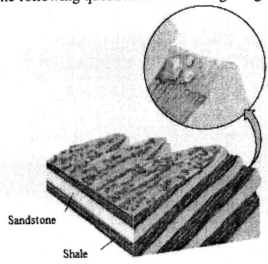

Sandstone

Shale

31. If the rock package represented in the cross section above were to be eroded, what type of landform would it most likely create?
    A) cuesta   B) hogback   C) mesa   D) mountain
    Ans: A   Page: 416

Use the following to answer question 32:

The following question refers to the geologic cross-section below.

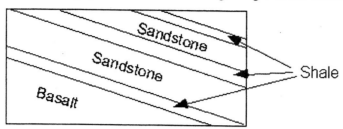

32. Which of the rock units in the diagram above is most easily eroded?
    A) basalt
    B) sandstone
    C) shale
    D) Basalt, sandstone, and shale are equally erodable.
    Ans: C   Page: 417

33. What is the geologic term for an asymmetric ridge where gently dipping beds of erosion-resistant rocks are undercut by erosion of a weaker underlying bed?
    A) cuesta   B) hogback   C) mesa   D) syncline
    Ans: A   Page: 416

34. Which of the following is an example of an erosional landform?
    A) cuesta   B) floodplain   C) moraine   D) sand dune
    Ans: A   Page: 416

35. What type of topography consists of deep gullies resulting from the rapid erosion of easily eroded shales and clays?
    A) badland topography   C) karst topography
    B) cuesta topography   D) plateau topography
    Ans: A   Page: 416

36. Which of the following would lead to the formation of badland?
    A) rapid erosion of metamorphic rocks   C) slow erosion of metamorphic rocks
    B) rapid erosion of sedimentary rocks   D) slow erosion of sedimentary rocks
    Ans: B   Page: 416

37. Which of the following states contains badlands?
    A) Alaska   B) Florida   C) Massachusetts   D) South Dakota
    Ans: D   Page: 416

38. Cuestas and hogbacks are formed by erosion of _____.
    A) flat-lying basaltic lava flows
    B) granites and diorites
    C) stratovolcanoes
    D) tilted sedimentary rocks
    Ans: D   Page: 416-417

Use the following to answer question 39:

39. If the rock package represented in the cross-sectional diagram above were to be eroded, what type of landform would it most likely create?
    A) cuesta B) hogback C) mesa D) mountain
    Ans: B   Page: 417

40. Which of the following affects landscape evolution?
    A) bedrock type B) climate C) tectonics D) all of the above
    Ans: D   Page: 417

41. What type of process produces an effect that slows down the original action and stabilizes the process at a slower rate?
    A) constructive correlation
    B) destructive correlation
    C) negative-feedback process
    D) positive-feedback process
    Ans: C   Page: 417

42. Which of the following best describes the effect of tectonic uplift on the erosion rate?
    A) Tectonic uplift decreases the erosion rate.
    B) Tectonic uplift increases the erosion rate.
    C) Tectonic uplift can either decrease or increase the erosion rate.
    D) Tectonic uplift does not affect the erosion rate.
    Ans: B   Alternative Location: Online quizzing   Page: 418-419

43. Which of the following Cenozoic epochs was the warmest?
    A) Eocene B) Miocene C) Oligocene D) Pleistocene
    Ans: A   Page: 420

44. Which of the following is the highest and largest topographic feature on Earth?
    A) the Alps
    B) the Andes Mountains
    C) the Rocky Mountains
    D) the Tibetan Plateau
    Ans: D   Page: 420

45. In which of the following regions will erosion rates be highest?
    A) high elevation and high relief
    B) high elevation and low relief
    C) low elevation and high relief
    D) low elevation and low relief
    Ans: A   Page: 421

46. The progression from young, high, rugged mountains to older, worn-down, rounded hills is called _____.
    A) Davis' cycle of erosion
    B) the hydrologic cycle
    C) the rock cycle
    D) the Wilson cycle
    Ans: A   Page: 422

47. How rapid are tectonic uplift rates in active mountain ranges?
    A) approximately 1-10 millimeters per year
    B) approximately 1-10 centimeters per year
    C) approximately 10-100 centimeters per year
    D) approximately 1-10 meters per year
    Ans: A   Page: 423

48. Which of the following radioactive isotopes is generated by cosmic waves that penetrate the upper meter of soil and rock?
    A) beryllium-10   B) carbon-14   C) potassium-40   D) uranium-235
    Ans: A   Page: 423

49. Who proposed that landscape evolution can achieve a dynamic equilibrium where uplift and erosion rates are sustained for a long period of time?
    A) Charles Darwin   B) John Hack   C) Walther Penck   D) William Davis
    Ans: B   Page: 423

50. How rapid are stream erosion rates in the Himalayas based on radioactive dating?
    A) 2 to 12 mm/yr   B) 2 to 12 cm/yr   C) 2 to 12 m/yr   D) 2 to 12 km/yr
    Ans: A   Page: 423

Chapter 19: Earthquakes

1. The amount of ground displacement in an earthquake is called the _____.
   A) dip B) epicenter C) focus D) slip
   Ans: D   Page: 430

2. What does the elastic rebound theory describe?
   A) the build-up and release of stress during an earthquake
   B) the fluctuations in groundwater prior to an earthquake
   C) the formation of mountain ranges by successive earthquakes
   D) the uplift of the crust in response to erosion
   Ans: A   Page: 430

Use the following to answer questions 3-6:

The following questions refer to the cross section below.

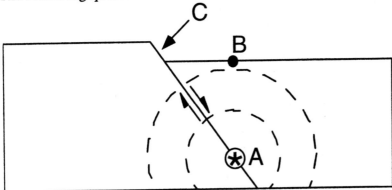

3. Point A, where slip initiated during the earthquake, is called the _____.
   A) dip B) epicenter C) focus D) strike
   Ans: C   Page: 430

4. Point B is called the earthquake _____.
   A) dip B) epicenter C) focus D) strike
   Ans: B   Page: 430

5. Which of the following forces likely generated the earthquake depicted in the diagram?
   A) compression forces B) shearing forces C) tension forces D) torsional forces
   Ans: B   Page: 438

6. What type of faulting is illustrated in the cross section above?
   A) normal faulting
   B) reverse faulting
   C) left-lateral strike-slip faulting
   D) right-lateral strike-slip faulting
   Ans: A   Page: 438

7. What is the <u>maximum</u> amount of slip on a fault during an earthquake?
   A) about 1 meters
   B) about 10 meters
   C) about 100 meters
   D) about 1000 meters
   Ans: B   Page: 430

8. Which of the following statements regarding aftershocks is <u>true</u>?
   A) The number and sizes of aftershocks <u>both</u> decrease with time.
   B) The number of aftershocks decreases with time, while the sizes of aftershocks increase with time.
   C) The number of aftershocks increases with time, while the sizes of aftershocks decrease with time.
   D) The number and sizes of aftershocks <u>both</u> increase with time.
   Ans: A   Page: 430-431

Use the following to answer questions 9-12:

The following questions refer to the seismographic recording (seismogram) of an earthquake below:

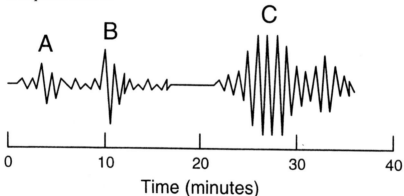

9. What causes the up-and-down wiggles on the seismogram?
   A) electromagnetic pulses
   B) ground vibrations
   C) tsunami waves
   D) variations in air pressure
   Ans: B   Page: 431

10. Which sets of waves travel through the Earth's interior?
    A) set A   B) set B   C) sets A and B   D) sets A, B, and C
    Ans: C   Page: 432

11. Which set of waves are most likely surface waves?
    A) set A   B) set B   C) set C   D) Sets A, B, and C are all surface waves.
    Ans: C   Page: 433

12. Approximately how far away from the seismograph station was the earthquake?
    A) 5 km   B) 50 km   C) 500 km   D) 5000 km
    Ans: D   Page: 434

13. Which of the following types of seismic waves arrive at a seismograph first?
    A) P waves
    B) S waves
    C) surface waves
    D) All of these waves arrive at the same time.
    Ans: A   Page: 431

14. Which of the following correctly lists the order in which seismic waves arrive at a seismograph station?
    A) P waves → surface waves → S waves   C) S waves → P waves → surface waves
    B) P waves → S waves → surface waves   D) surface waves → P waves → S waves
    Ans: B   Page: 432

15. If an earthquake occurred in Seattle, Washington, how long would it take for the first seismic waves to arrive at a seismograph station in Miami, Florida, approximately 5000 kilometers away?
    A) about 8 seconds   B) about 8 minutes   C) about 8 hours   D) about 8 days
    Ans: B   Page: 434

16. What type of seismic waves are S waves?
    A) compressional waves   B) shear waves   C) surface waves   D) tsunamis
    Ans: B   Page: 432

17. Which of the following types of seismic waves are the slowest?
    A) P waves
    B) S waves
    C) surface waves
    D) P waves, S waves, and surface waves all travel at the same speed.
    Ans: C   Page: 432

18. Which of the following types of waves is a compressional sound wave?
    A) P wave   B) S wave   C) surface wave   D) all of the above
    Ans: A   Page: 432

19. How do rock particles move during the passage of an S wave through the rock?
    A) back and forth parallel to the direction of wave travel
    B) back and forth at right angles to the direction of wave travel
    C) in a rolling circular motion
    D) in a rolling elliptical motion
    Ans: B   Page: 433

20. As the distance to an earthquake increases, _____.
    A) the elapsed time before the P waves arrive decreases
    B) the elapsed time before the S waves arrive increases
    C) the amount of ground shaking increases
    D) the time between the arrival of the P and S waves decreases
    Ans: B   Page: 434

21. What is the moment magnitude of an earthquake proportional to?
    A) the area of the fault break
    B) the seismic energy released during the rupture
    C) both A and B
    D) neither A nor B
    Ans: C   Page: 435

22. Who developed the procedure used to measure the size of an earthquake?
    A) Henri Darcy   B) Charles Darwin   C) James Hutton   D) Charles Richter
    Ans: D   Page: 435

23. An earthquake's Richter magnitude is based on _____.
    A) the amount of energy released during an earthquake
    B) the amount of ground movement caused by seismic waves
    C) the distance between the earthquake and the seismograph station
    D) the observed effects on people and structures
    Ans: B   Page: 435

24. The ground motion during a Richter magnitude 8 earthquake is _____ times greater than the ground motion during a Richter magnitude 6 earthquake.
    A) 2 B) 10   C) 100   D) 1000
    Ans: C   Page: 435

25. How many seismograph stations are needed to locate the epicenter of an earthquake?
    A) 1 B) 2   C) 3   D) 4
    Ans: C   Page: 434

26. The energy released during a magnitude 8 earthquake is approximately _____ times large than the energy released during a magnitude 6 earthquake.
    A) 2 B) 10   C) 100   D) 1000
    Ans: D   Page: 436

27. Approximately how many magnitude 7 earthquakes occur each year?
    A) 1   B) 10   C) 100   D) 1000
    Ans: B   Page: 436

28. Which of the following earthquakes was the largest recorded earthquake?
    A) 1906 San Francisco, California   C) 1960 Chile
    B) 1923 Tokyo, Japan   D) 1976 Tangshan, China
    Ans: C   Page: 436

29. Which of the following events released the most energy?
    A) the eruption of Mt. St. Helens
    B) the explosion of the Hiroshima atomic bomb
    C) the 1964 Alaska earthquake
    D) <u>All</u> of these released similar amounts of energy.
    Ans: C   Page: 436

30. Which of the following measurements collected from seismograph stations gives scientists information regarding the <u>type of faulting</u> that occurred during an earthquake?
    A) the amount of slip
    B) the amplitude of the ground shaking
    C) the first motion of the P waves
    D) the time interval between the arrival of the P and S waves
    Ans: C   Page: 437

31. Which of the following statements about earthquakes is <u>true</u>?
    A) Earthquakes can be caused by normal, reverse, and strike-slip faulting.
    B) Most earthquakes occur in intraplate settings.
    C) S waves travel faster than both P waves and surface waves.
    D) The time and location of most major earthquakes can be predicted several days in advance.
    Ans: A   Page: 438

32. Shallow earthquakes, less than 20 km deep, are associated with _____.
    A) convergent plate boundaries   C) transform plate boundaries
    B) divergent plate boundaries   D) <u>all</u> of the above
    Ans: D   Page: 440

33. Which of the following countries has the <u>least</u> risk of earthquakes?
    A) Australia   B) China   C) Japan   D) United Sates
    Ans: A   Page: 440

34. Earthquakes that originate at depths greater than 100 km are associated with _____ plate boundaries.
   A) convergent
   B) divergent
   C) transform
   D) convergent, divergent, and transform
   Ans: A   Page: 440

Use the following to answer questions 35-36:

The following questions refer to the map of a mid-ocean ridge depicted below.

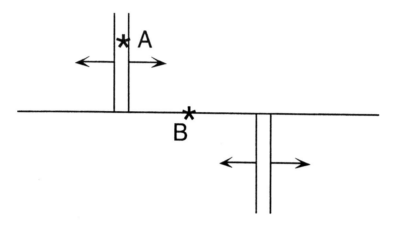

35. What type of earthquakes would most likely occur at point A?
   A) shallow-focus earthquakes caused by normal faulting
   B) shallow-focus earthquakes caused by strike-slip faulting
   C) shallow-focus earthquakes caused by thrust faulting
   D) deep-focus earthquakes caused by thrust faulting
   Ans: A   Page: 441

36. What type of earthquakes would most likely occur at point B?
   A) shallow-focus earthquakes caused by normal faulting
   B) shallow-focus earthquakes caused by strike-slip faulting
   C) shallow-focus earthquakes caused by thrust faulting
   D) deep-focus earthquakes caused by thrust faulting
   Ans: B   Page: 441

37. What type of faulting would be <u>least</u> likely to occur along the mid-Atlantic ridge?
   A) normal faulting
   B) reverse faulting
   C) strike-slip faulting
   D) Normal, reverse, and strike-slip faulting are <u>all</u> likely to occur.
   Ans: B   Page: 441

38. What type of fault is the San Andreas fault in California?
    A) normal fault
    B) reverse fault
    C) left-lateral strike-slip fault
    D) right-lateral strike-slip fault
    Ans: D   Page: 441

39. What was the approximate magnitude of the 1994 Northridge earthquake in Los Angeles?
    A) magnitude 6   B) magnitude 7   C) magnitude 8   D) magnitude 9
    Ans: B   Page: 442

40. Which of the following recent earthquakes killed the most people?
    A) the 1989 Loma Prieta earthquake, northern California
    B) the 1994 Northridge earthquake, southern California
    C) the 1995 Kobe earthquake, Japan
    D) the 2001 Gujarat earthquake, India
    Ans: D   Page: 443

41. Which of the following statements about tsunamis is false?
    A) An early warning system for tsunamis has been developed for the Pacific region.
    B) Tsunamis are produced by tidal forces, which is why they are also called tidal waves.
    C) Tsunamis can reach heights in excess of 20 meters when they reach the shore.
    D) Tsunamis travel slower than P and S waves.
    Ans: B   Page: 446

42. How fast do tsunamis travel across the ocean?
    A) up to 5 kilometers per hour
    B) up to 60 kilometers per hour
    C) up to 800 kilometers per hour
    D) up to 10,000 kilometers per hour
    Ans: C   Page: 446

43. Which of the following statements is most accurate?
    A) Both seismic hazards and seismic risks can be reduced.
    B) Seismic hazards can be reduced, but seismic risks cannot.
    C) Seismic risks can be reduced, but seismic hazards cannot.
    D) Neither seismic hazards nor seismic risks can be reduced.
    Ans: C   Page: 446

44. Which of the following regions has the greatest seismic hazard?
    A) central U.S.   B) northeastern U.S.   C) southeastern U.S.   D) western U.S.
    Ans: D   Page: 446-447

45. Which of the following pieces of evidence recently led scientists to propose that great earthquakes occur in Oregon, Washington, and British Columbia every 500-600 years?
    A) dramatic increases in the number of small (M=6) earthquakes
    B) geologic records of flooded, dead coastal forests
    C) groundwater records showing dramatic fluctuations in the water table
    D) seismograph records of great earthquakes that were previously underestimated
    Ans: B   Page: 447-448

46. Tsunamis can be generated by _____.
    A) undersea earthquakes   C) the eruption of an oceanic volcano
    B) undersea landslides   D) <u>all</u> of the above
    Ans: D   Page: 449

47. How much warning could a "real-time earthquake warning system" provide before destructive seismic waves arrive?
    A) about a minute   B) about a hour   C) about a day   D) about a week
    Ans: A   Page: 450

48. Which of the following specifies the level of ground shaking that a structure must be able to withstand?
    A) building code   B) elastic rebound   C) intensity scale   D) magnitude scale
    Ans: A   Page: 450

49. Which of the following statements best describes the current state of earthquake prediction?
    A) Scientists can accurately predict the time and location of almost all earthquakes.
    B) Scientists can accurately predict the time and location of about 50% of all earthquakes.
    C) Scientists can accurately predict when an earthquake will occur, but not where.
    D) Scientists <u>cannot</u> yet accurately predict most earthquakes.
    Ans: D   Page: 452

50. In southern California, great earthquakes occur on the San Andreas approximately every _____ years.
    A) 1 to 2   B) 5 to 10   C) 25 to 75   D) 150 to 300
    Ans: D   Page: 452

Chapter 20: Evolution of the Continents

1. Oceanic crust provides a record of about ___ of Earth's history.
   A) 5%   B) 25%   C) 75%   D) 95%
   Ans: A   Page: 457

2. The oldest continental crust is approximately ___ of the age of the Earth.
   A) 5%   B) 25%   C) 50%   D) 90%
   Ans: D   Page: 457

3. What mountain chain runs along the eastern margin of North America?
   A) Andes   B) Appalachians   C) Caledonides   D) Cordillera
   Ans: B   Page: 458

4. The oldest rocks tend to be found _____.
   A) along the margins of continents   C) in the interior of continents
   B) along the margins of ocean basins   D) in the interiors of ocean basins
   Ans: C   Page: 458

5. Where are the oldest rocks in North America located?
   A) in the Appalachian Mountains   C) in the Canadian Shield
   B) in the Basin and Range province   D) in the Rocky Mountains
   Ans: C   Page: 458

Use the following to answer questions 6-9:

The following questions refer to the map of North America depicted below.

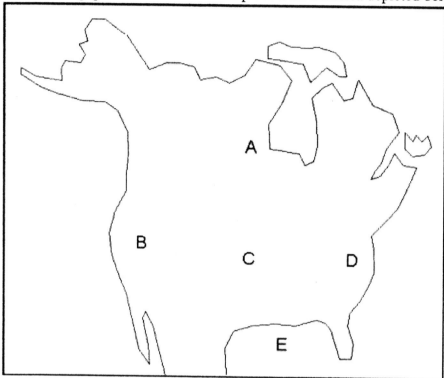

6. Which region consists of folded and faulted rocks that formed during the Paleozoic Era?
   A) region A   B) region B   C) region C   D) region D
   Ans: D   Page: 458

7. Which region represents the North American Cordillera?
   A) region A   B) region B   C) region C   D) region D
   Ans: B   Page: 458

8. Which region is characterized by flat-lying sedimentary rocks at the surface?
   A) region A   B) region B   C) region C   D) region D
   Ans: C   Page: 458

9. Which region contains the thickest sedimentary deposits?
   A) region A   B) region C   C) region D   D) region E
   Ans: D   Page: 458

10. Which of the following is <u>not</u> a common rock type in the Canadian Shield?
    A) gneisses
    B) granitic rocks
    C) highly deformed metamorphosed volcanic rocks
    D) undeformed sedimentary rocks
    Ans: D   Page: 458

11. In which of the following settings were most of the rocks of the interior platform of North America deposited?
    A) in a continental rift
    B) in a deep ocean basin
    C) in an extensive shallow sea
    D) in a volcanic island arc
    Ans: C   Page: 459

12. What type of geologic contact separates the rocks of the Canadian Shield from the rocks of the Great Plains? (Hint: Consider the type and age of the rocks found in each area.)
    A) intrusive contact   B) strike-slip fault   C) thrust fault   D) unconformity
    Ans: D   Page: 459

13. How thick is the sequence of sedimentary rocks that underlies the Great Plains?
    A) several tens of meters thick
    B) several hundreds of meters thick
    C) several kilometers thick
    D) several tens of kilometers thick
    Ans: C   Page: 459

14. Which of the following physiographic regions in the Appalachian Mountains is the most intensely deformed?
    A) Appalachian plateau
    B) Blue Ridge province
    C) Piedmont
    D) Valley and Ridge Province
    Ans: C   Page: 460

15. The North American Cordillera formed over a period of _____.
    A) 2 million years   B) 10 million years   C) 50 million years   D) 200 million years
    Ans: D   Page: 462

16. Why is the North American Cordillera topographically higher than the Appalachians?
    A) because the Appalachians have undergone less erosion
    B) because the Cordillera formed by continent-continent collision
    C) because the main orogeny in the Cordillera was more recent
    D) because the spreading rate of the East Pacific Rise is greater than the spreading rate of the Mid-Atlantic Ridge
    Ans: C   Page: 462

17. How far do continental deformation zones, like the Cordilleran orogenic belt, extend from a plate boundary?
    A) a few kilometers
    B) a few tens of kilometers
    C) a few hundreds of kilometers
    D) a thousand kilometers
    Ans: D   Page: 462

18. In which of the following regions would you expect to find the thickest sequence of sedimentary rocks?
    A) along mid-ocean ridges
    B) in the middle of the ocean basin, away from a ridge
    C) on continental platforms
    D) on continental shelves
    Ans: D   Page: 463

19. Which of the following processes is responsible for the topography of the Basin and Range province in western North America?
    A) normal faulting   B) strike-slip faulting   C) thrust faulting   D) upwarping
    Ans: A   Page: 463

20. The present-day topography of the Basin and Range province formed during _____ time.
    A) Cenozoic   B) Mesozoic   C) Paleozoic   D) Precambrian
    Ans: A   Page: 463

21. Which of the following regions contains numerous fault-block mountain ranges?
    A) the Appalachians
    B) the Basin and Range province
    C) the Canadian Shield
    D) the Great Plains
    Ans: B   Page: 463

22. Which of the following geologic events occurred most recently?
    A) collision of Laurasia and Gondwana
    B) faulting of the Basin and Range province
    C) initial rifting of the Atlantic Ocean
    D) magmatism in the Canadian Shield
    Ans: B   Page: 463

23. What are cratons made up of?
    A) orogens and platforms
    B) orogens and shields
    C) platforms and shields
    D) orogens, platforms, and shields
    Ans: C   Page: 464

24. What is meant by the tectonic age of a region?
    A) the oldest rocks in the region
    B) the oldest major deformation event in the region
    C) the youngest rocks in the region
    D) the youngest major deformation event in the region
    Ans: D   Page: 465

25. Over the past 4 billion years, which of the following best describes how the volume of the continents has changed?
    A) The volume of the continents has decreased by about 100 cubic kilometers per year.
    B) The volume of the continents has remained approximately constant.
    C) The volume of the continents has increased by about 2 cubic kilometers per year.
    D) The volume of the continents has increased by about 100 cubic kilometers per year.
    Ans: C   Page: 466

26. In which of the following regions is new material currently being added to the crust?
    A) Appalachian Mountains   C) Cascade Range
    B) Canadian Shield   D) Rocky Mountains
    Ans: C   Page: 466

27. Which of the following best describes the type of rocks that make up Wrangellia, an exotic terrane in western North America.
    A) continental fragment   B) island arc   C) oceanic plateau   D) all of the above
    Ans: C   Page: 467

28. Which of the following accretion processes has not occurred along western North America?
    A) accretion along a transform fault   C) accretion of a continental fragment
    B) accretion during continent collision   D) accretion of an island arc
    Ans: B   Page: 467-469

29. What is an orogeny?
    A) a broad exposure of deformed metamorphic and igneous rocks
    B) a general term for mountain-building processes
    C) a special type of reverse fault
    D) a theory that explains the uplift of continents after large ice sheets melt
    Ans: B   Alternative Location: Online quizzing   Page: 468

30. Which of the following mountain belts formed as a result of a collision between two continents?
    A) Appalachians   B) Himalayas   C) Urals   D) all of these
    Ans: D   Page: 469-473

31. The Himalayas consist primarily of _____.
    A) basaltic lava flows and gabbroic intrusions
    B) gently folded sedimentary rocks
    C) granitic to dioritic plutons and related volcanic rocks
    D) thrust sheets of deformed and metamorphosed sedimentary rocks
    Ans: D   Page: 470

32. How thick is the crust of the Tibetan plateau?
    A) 10-20 km thick   C) 60-70 km thick
    B) 30-40 km thick   D) 100-150 km thick
    Ans: C   Page: 472

33. The Himalayas began to form approximately _____ when the Indian subcontinent
    began to collide with Tibet.
    A) 5 million years ago   C) 500 million years ago
    B) 50 million years ago   D) 5 billion years ago
    Ans: B   Page: 470

34. Which of the following statements is <u>true</u>?
    A) India is colliding with Asia at a rate of about 4 millimeters per year.
    B) India is colliding with Asia at a rate of about 4 centimeters per year.
    C) India is colliding with Asia at a rate of about 4 meters per year.
    D) India is no longer colliding with Asia.
    Ans: B   Page: 472

Use the following to answer questions 35-36:

The following questions refer to the cross section of a continental collision depicted
below.

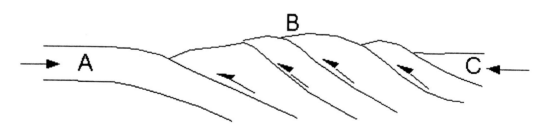

35. What type of faults are depicted in the cross section?
    A) normal faults   C) thrust faults
    B) strike-slip faults   D) cannot tell from the information given
    Ans: C   Page: 470

36. If "B" represents the Himalayas today, then _____.
    A) plate A is Asia and plate C is Europe C) plate A is Asia and plate C is India
    B) plate A is India and plate C is Asia D) plate A is Europe and plate C is Asia
    Ans: B   Page: 471

37. Prior to the collision of India and Asia, oceanic crust was subducted beneath

    _____ .
    A) Asia   B) India   C) both Asia and India   D) neither Asia nor India
    Ans: A   Page: 471

38. The main thrust sheets in the Himalayas were transported _____.
    A) northward   B) southward   C) eastward   D) westward
    Ans: B   Page: 471

    Use the following to answer questions 39-40:

    The following questions refer to the events in the development of the Himalayas listed
    below:

    I. formation of the Main Boundary fault
    II. formation of the Main Central thrust
    III. collision of the Indian and Eurasian continents
    IV. formation of a volcanic arc on southern edge of Eurasia

39. Which of events listed above occurred before the collision of India and Eurasia?
    A) event I   B) event II   C) event IV   D) events I, II, and IV
    Ans: C   Page: 471

40. Which of the following correctly lists the sequence of events that led to the development
    of the Himalayas?
    A) I → II → III   B) II → I → III   C) III → I → II   D) III → II → I
    Ans: D   Page: 471

41. When did the three main orogenies that formed the Appalachian Mountains occur?
    A) during the Cenozoic   C) during the Paleozoic
    B) during the Mesozoic   D) during the Precambrian
    Ans: C   Page: 472

42. Which of the following mountain chains was the result of a continental collision during
    the assembly of the supercontinent Pangaea?
    A) Andes   B) Appalachians   C) Cordillera   D) Himalayas
    Ans: B   Page: 472

43. Which of the following orogenies represents the final assembly of Pangaea?
    A) Acadian orogeny
    B) Appalachian orogeny
    C) Caledonian orogeny
    D) Taconic orogeny
    Ans: B   Page: 472-473

44. Which of the following sequences describes the Wilson cycle?
    I.   continent-continent collision
    II.   continental rifting
    III. sea-floor spreading
    IV.   subduction
    A) I → IV → II → III
    B) II → III → IV → I
    C) III → I → IV → II
    D) IV → II → III → IV
    Ans: B   Page: 474-475

45. Which of the following terms refers to the gradual vertical movements of the crust without significant deformation?
    A) accretion   B) epeirogeny   C) orogeny   D) rejuvenation
    Ans: B   Page: 476

46. Which of the following regions is an example of an epeirogenic uplift?
    A) Appalachian Mountains
    B) Colorado Plateau
    C) Rocky Mountains
    D) Sierra Nevada
    Ans: B   Page: 476

47. Which of the following is not a cause of epeirogenic movement?
    A) glacial rebound
    B) lithospheric heating
    C) lithospheric cooling
    D) ocean-continent convergence
    Ans: D   Page: 476-477

48. When did plate tectonics and the Wilson cycle begin?
    A) approximately 0.5 billion years ago
    B) approximately 1.0 billion years ago
    C) approximately 2.5 billion years ago
    D) approximately 4.0 billion years ago
    Ans: C   Page: 477

49. Which of the following regions has the thickest lithosphere?
    A) Archean cratons
    B) Cenozoic orogenic belts
    C) oceans
    D) Paleozoic orogenic belts
    Ans: A   Page: 479

50. Which of the following statements about cratonic keels is <u>true</u>?
    A) Cratonic keels are <u>cooler</u> than normal mantle lithosphere, but have the <u>same</u> chemical composition.
    B) Cratonic keels are <u>cooler</u> than normal mantle lithosphere and have a <u>different</u> chemical composition.
    C) Cratonic keels are <u>warmer</u> than normal mantle lithosphere, but have the <u>same</u> chemical composition.
    D) Cratonic keels are <u>warmer</u> than normal mantle lithosphere and have a <u>different</u> chemical composition.

    Ans: B   Page: 479-480

Chapter 21: Exploring Earth's Interior

1. What is the approximate distance from the surface to the center of the Earth?
   A) 700 km   B) 2900 km   C) 6400 km   D) 24,000 km
   Ans: C   Page: 483

2. How fast do P waves travel through granite?
   A) 4 kilometers per second
   B) 6 kilometers per second
   C) 8 kilometers per second
   D) 12 kilometers per second
   Ans: B   Page: 484

Use the following to answer questions 3-4:

The following questions refer to the cross section through the Earth depicted below.

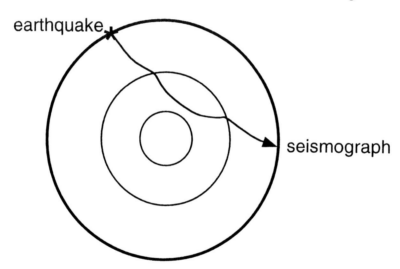

3. What type of seismic wave is depicted by the ray path in the diagram?
   A) a P wave   B) an S wave   C) a surface wave   D) <u>all</u> of the above
   Ans: A   Page: 485

4. The two kinks in the seismic wave path are examples of seismic _____.
   A) isostasy   B) reflection   C) refraction   D) tomography
   Ans: C   Page: 485

5. The S-wave shadow zone extends from _____ to 180° angular distance from the earthquake focus.
   A) 45°   B) 75°   C) 105°   D) 145°
   Ans: C   Page: 485

6. Which of the following statements is <u>true</u>?
   A) Liquids do <u>not</u> transmit P waves.
   B) P-wave velocities are greater in the core than in the mantle.
   C) Seismic waves follow straight paths through the interior of the Earth.
   D) The S-wave shadow zone is larger than the P-wave shadow zone.
   Ans: D   Page: 485

Use the following to answer questions 7-9:

The following questions refer to the cross section of the Earth depicted below.

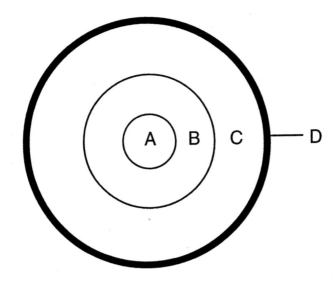

7. Which region in the Earth is molten?
   A) region A   B) region B   C) region C   D) region D
   Ans: B   Page: 486, 491

8. Which region in the Earth consists primarily of solid iron?
   A) region A   B) region B   C) region C   D) region D
   Ans: A   Page: 490-491

9. In which region of the Earth is conduction the dominant heat transfer mechanism?
   A) region A   B) region B   C) region C   D) region D
   Ans: D   Page: 491

10. Which of the following seismic waves will arrive at a seismograph first?
    A) P   B) S   C) PP   D) SS
    Ans: A   Page: 486

11. Which layer in the Earth does <u>not</u> transmit S waves?
    A) crust   B) inner core   C) mantle   D) outer core
    Ans: D   Page: 487

12. Where do P waves travel fastest?
    A) in the upper mantle
    B) in the lower mantle
    C) in the outer core
    D) in the inner core
    Ans: B   Page: 487

13. Continental crust beneath mountains can be up to ___ kilometers thick
    A) 10   B) 40   C) 70   D) 100
    Ans: C   Page: 487

14. How thick is the oceanic crust?
    A) approximately 7 km
    B) approximately 35 km
    C) approximately 70 km
    D) approximately 240 km
    Ans: A   Page: 487

15. The oceanic crust consists mostly of _____.
    A) felsic rocks   B) mafic rocks   C) sedimentary rocks   D) ultramafic rocks
    Ans: B   Page: 487

16. Which of the following correctly lists the three rock types in order of increasing P-wave velocity?
    A) gabbro → granite → peridotite
    B) granite → gabbro → peridotite
    C) granite → peridotite → gabbro
    D) peridotite → gabbro → granite
    Ans: B   Page: 487

17. Which of the following statements about the Moho (Mohovoricic discontinuity) is false?
    A) The Moho marks the top of a partially molten layer.
    B) The Moho separates denser rocks below from less dense rocks above.
    C) The Moho separates the crust from the mantle.
    D) The speed of seismic waves increases as they pass down through the Moho.
    Ans: A   Page: 487

18. Which of the following statements is false?
    A) P waves travel slower in the crust than in the mantle.
    B) The crust is denser than the mantle.
    C) The crust-mantle boundary is called the Mohorovicic discontinuity.
    D) The oceanic crust consists of basalt and gabbro.
    Ans: B   Page: 487

19. Which of the following marks the boundary between the crust and the mantle?
    A) a decrease in P-wave velocity and a change in rock type
    B) an increase in P-wave velocity and a change in rock type
    C) a decrease in P-wave velocity, but no change in rock type
    D) an increase in P-wave velocity, but no change in rock type
    Ans: B   Page: 487

20. What principle is based on the continents being less dense than the underlying mantle?
    A) epeirogeny   B) isostasy   C) superposition   D) tomography
    Ans: B   Page: 487

21. Why is the average elevation of the continents higher than the average elevation of the seafloor?
    A) because melting of large ice caps has caused isostatic rebound of the continents
    B) because oceanic crust is composed of denser rocks than the continental crust
    C) because the continents are supported by upwelling mantle currents
    D) because subduction pulls down the seafloor
    Ans: B   Page: 487-488

22. After melting of a continental ice cap, the surface of the continent will tend to _____.
    A) rise
    B) sink
    C) rise or sink depending on the thickness of the ice cap
    D) remain the same
    Ans: A   Page: 489

23. Which of the following regions in the Earth consists primarily of olivine and pyroxene?
    A) the crust   B) the upper mantle   C) the lower mantle   D) the inner core
    Ans: B   Page: 488

24. How thick is average lithosphere?
    A) 25 km   B) 100 km   C) 250 km   D) 1000 km
    Ans: B   Page: 488

25. Which of the following statements about the asthenosphere is <u>false</u>?
    A) The asthenosphere lies beneath the lithosphere.
    B) The asthenosphere is stronger than the lithosphere.
    C) The asthenosphere rises close to the surface beneath mid-ocean ridges.
    D) The asthenosphere is partially molten.
    Ans: B   Page: 488, 490

26. The boundary between the mantle and the core lies at a depth of approximately _____.
    A) 300 kilometers   C) 3000 kilometers
    B) 1000 kilometers   D) 10,000 kilometers
    Ans: C   Page: 490

27. Which of the following regions is the source of most basaltic magma?
    A) asthenosphere   B) lithosphere   C) lower mantle   D) outer core
    Ans: A   Page: 490

28. What causes the sharp increases in the velocity of S waves at 400 and 670 kilometers depth in the mantle?
    A) changes in the composition of the mantle
    B) changes in the mineral structures
    C) changes in the pressure of the mantle
    D) changes in the temperature of the mantle
    Ans: B   Page: 490

29. At what depth does the transition from the upper mantle to the lower mantle occur?
    A) approximately 100 kilometers   C) approximately 3000 kilometers
    B) approximately 700 kilometers   D) approximately 5000 kilometers
    Ans: A   Page: 490

30. What element makes up most of the Earth's core?
    A) iron   B) oxygen   C) magnesium   D) silicon
    Ans: A   Page: 490

31. According to a recent hypothesis, from which boundary do mantle plumes that feed hot spots originate?
    A) the asthenosphere-lithosphere boundary
    B) the core-mantle boundary
    C) the crust-mantle boundary
    D) the inner core–outer core boundary
    Ans: B   Page: 490

32. Which of the following statements about the Earth's core is <u>true</u>?
    A) The inner core and the outer core are both liquid.
    B) The inner core and the outer core are both solid.
    C) The inner core is liquid and the outer core is solid.
    D) The inner core is solid and the outer core is liquid.
    Ans: D   Page: 490-491

33. The mechanical transfer of heat by vibration of atoms and molecules is called _____.
    A) conduction   B) convection   C) magnetism   D) radiation
    Ans: A   Page: 491

34. What drives plate tectonics?
    A) erosion   B) solar energy   C) thermal conduction   D) thermal convection
    Ans: D   Page: 492

35. Over geologic time, most of the heat lost from the Earth's interior has been transported by _____.
    A) conduction   B) convection   C) radioactive decay   D) solar radiation
    Ans: B   Page: 492

36. In a deep mine, temperatures increase at the rate of _____.
    A) approximately 2.5 °C per kilometer   C) approximately 250 °C per kilometer
    B) approximately 25 °C per kilometer   D) approximately 2500 °C per kilometer
    Ans: B   Page: 492

37. Which of the following regions is hottest?
    A) crust   B) inner core   C) mantle   D) outer core
    Ans: B   Page: 493

38. The temperature at the center of the Earth is approximately _____.
    A) 200 °C   B) 500 °C   C) 2000 °C   D) 5000 °C
    Ans: D   Page: 493

39. Seismic wave speeds increase with _____.
    A) decreasing density and temperature
    B) decreasing density and increasing temperature
    C) increasing density and decreasing temperature
    D) increasing density and temperature
    Ans: C   Page: 494

40. Seismic tomography has revealed that seismic waves in the uppermost mantle are
    relatively _____.
    A) fast beneath both mid-ocean ridges and subduction zones
    B) fast beneath mid-ocean ridges and slow beneath subduction zones
    C) slow beneath mid-ocean ridges and fast beneath subduction zones
    D) slow beneath both mid-ocean ridges and subduction zones
    Ans: C   Page: 494

41. Based on seismic tomographic images, how deep do subducting slabs extend?
    A) to the crust-mantle boundary
    B) to the upper mantle-lower mantle boundary
    C) to the core-mantle boundary
    D) to the inner core-outer core boundary
    Ans: C   Page: 494

42. What cause large-scale variations in the Earth's geoid?
    A) variations in gravity   C) variations in radioactivity
    B) variations in magnetism   D) variations in solar energy
    Ans: A   Page: 496

43. Who first proposed that the Earth acted as a large magnet whose field forces the needle
    of a magnetic compass to align north-south?
    A) Charles Darwin   B) William Gilbert   C) James Hutton   D) Charles Lyell
    Ans: B   Page: 497

44. Where is the Earth's magnetic field generated?
    A) in the crust   B) in the mantle   C) in the outer core   D) in the inner core
    Ans: C   Page: 498

45. Above what temperature do materials lose their permanent magnetism?
    A) 100 °C   B) 500 °C   C) 1000 °C   D) 5000 °C
    Ans: B   Page: 498

46. Approximately how often does the Earth's magnetic field reverse itself?
    A) every 50 years
    B) every 5000 years
    C) every 500,000 years
    D) every 50,000,000 years
    Ans: C   Page: 502

47. How much of the Earth's magnetic field can be described by a simple dipole?
    A) 10%   B) 25%   C) 75%   D) 90%
    Ans: D   Page: 499

48. Which of the following Earth systems powers the Earth's magnetic field?
    A) climate system
    B) geodynamo system
    C) plate tectonic system
    D) all of the above
    Ans: B   Page: 498

49. Which of the following processes is responsible for the recording of the magnetic reversals on the sea floor?
    A) depositional remanent magnetism
    B) metamorphic magnetism
    C) tectonosilicate magnetism
    D) thermoremanent magnetism
    Ans: D   Page: 501

50. When was there a 35 million year period during which the Earth's magnetic field did not undergo reversals?
    A) Cretaceous   B) Eocene   C) Miocene   D) Pliocene-Pleistocene
    Ans: A   Page: 503

Chapter 22: Energy and Material Resources from the Earth

1. Which of the following represents the total amount of oil that may become available for use in the future?
   A) reserves   B) reservoirs   C) resources   D) traps
   Ans: C   Page: 508

2. What is the leading source of energy used in the United States today?
   A) coal   B) natural gas   C) nuclear power   D) oil
   Ans: D   Page: 509

3. The world has the <u>least</u> amount of which of the following energy resources?
   A) coal
   B) oil
   C) uranium
   D) There are roughly equal amounts of each of these three energy resources.
   Ans: B   Page: 509

Use the following to answer questions 4-5:

The following questions refer to the histogram below depicting the percentages of various types of energy used in the United States today.

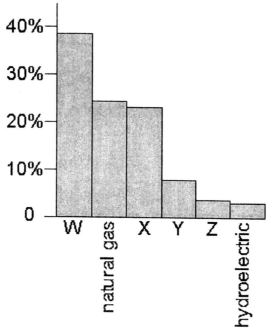

4. Which column represents oil?
   A) column W   B) column X   C) column Y   D) column Z
   Ans: A   Page: 509

5. Column X represents _____.
   A) coal   B) nuclear   C) oil   D) solar
   Ans: A   Page: 509

6. What percentage of the U.S. energy production is lost in distribution and inefficient use?
   A) 10%   B) 25%   C) 50%   D) 75%
   Ans: C   Page: 509

7. All oil traps contain a(n) _____.
   A) anticline   B) fault   C) impermeable layer   D) syncline
   Ans: C   Page: 510

Use the following to answer question 8:

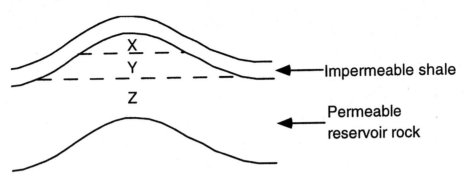

8. The cross section above depicts an oil trap, and X, Y, and Z represent three distinct fluid layers within the permeable reservoir rock. If the pore spaces in layer X contain natural gas, what will the pore spaces in layer Y likely contain?
   A) air   B) coal   C) oil   D) water
   Ans: C   Page: 511

9. When a fossil fuel is burned, we are releasing energy that was stored by _____.
   A) magmatism   B) photosynthesis   C) radioactivity   D) respiration
   Ans: B   Page: 510

10. Which of the following rock types would make the best oil reservoir?
    A) granite   B) salt   C) sandstone   D) shale
    Ans: C   Page: 510

11. Which of the following is least likely to create an oil trap?
    A) an anticline   B) a fault   C) a salt dome   D) a syncline
    Ans: D   Page: 511

12. Where are most of the world's known oil reserves located?
    A) Asia/Pacific   B) Middle East   C) North America   D) South America
    Ans: B   Page: 511-512

13. At the current rate of use, how long will the proven U.S. oil reserves last?
    A) 10 years   B) 40 years   C) 100 years   D) 400 years
    Ans: A   Page: 513

14. Burning of which of the following fuels produces the <u>least</u> amount of carbon dioxide per unit of energy?
   A) coal
   B) natural gas
   C) oil
   D) <u>All</u> of the above produce the same amount of carbon dioxide.
   Ans: B   Page: 514

15. When searching for coal deposits, geologists look for sedimentary rocks deposited in a
   _____.
   A) deep ocean environment   C) swampy environment
   B) desert environment   D) volcanic environment
   Ans: C   Page: 514

Use the following to answer questions 16-17:

The following questions refer to the diagram below.

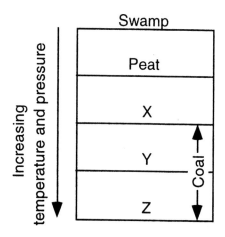

16. Which of the following correctly identifies X, Y, and Z?
   A) X = anthracite   Y = bituminous coal   Z = lignite
   B) X = lignite   Y = anthracite   Z = bituminous coal
   C) X = lignite   Y = bituminous coal   Z = anthracite
   D) X = bituminous coal   Y = anthracite   Z = lignite
   Ans: C   Page: 514-515

17. In addition to increasing pressure and temperature, the arrow to the left of the diagram represents increasing _____.
   A) carbon content   B) heat value   C) metamorphism   D) <u>all</u> of the above
   Ans: D   Page: 514-515

18. At the current rate of use in the United States, how long should U.S. coal resources last?
    A) a few years   C) a few hundreds of years
    B) a few tens of years   D) a few thousands of years
    Ans: C   Page: 515

19. Which of the following countries contains approximately 50% of the world's coal resources?
    A) Canada   B) China   C) former Soviet Union   D) United States
    Ans: C   Page: 515

20. Which of the following problems is associated with the burning of coal?
    A) acid rain   B) carbon dioxide   C) toxic ash   D) all of the above
    Ans: D   Page: 515

21. Nuclear energy is derived by the _____ of ^{235}U atoms.
    A) combustion   B) dissolution   C) fission   D) fusion
    Ans: C   Page: 516

22. Which of the following energy sources does not produce carbon dioxide?
    A) coal   B) natural gas   C) oil   D) uranium
    Ans: D   Page: 516

23. Approximately how many nuclear reactors are there in the United States?
    A) 20   B) 100   C) 500   D) 2000
    Ans: B   Page: 516

24. Which of the following energy sources does not generate greenhouse gases?
    A) coal   B) natural gas   C) nuclear   D) oil
    Ans: C   Page: 516

25. The primary barrier to using solar energy in the United States is that _____.
    A) solar power is not technically feasible
    B) solar power causes major pollution problems
    C) solar power is not economically competitive with other energy sources
    D) all of the above
    Ans: C   Page: 517

26. Hydroelectric energy provides about ___ of the energy consumed annually in the United States.
    A) 3%   B) 10%   C) 30%   D) 90%
    Ans: A   Page: 520

27. In what state is the world's largest supply of natural steam located?
    A) California   B) Florida   C) Pennsylvania   D) Texas
    Ans: A   Page: 520-521

28. Most metal ore deposits consist of _____.
    A) metal oxides   B) metal silicates   C) metal sulfides   D) native metals
    Ans: C   Page: 522

29. Which of the following metals has the lowest economical concentration factor?
    A) aluminum   B) copper   C) gold   D) iron
    Ans: A   Page: 523

30. Nearly 75% of which metal is currently recycled in the United States?
    A) aluminum   B) copper   C) iron   D) lead
    Ans: D   Page: 524

31. In 1992, $6.2 billion was paid to the federal government as rents and royalties for the use of federal lands. Which of the following industries was responsible for most of these payments?
    A) cattle ranching   B) mineral mining   C) oil and gas   D) timber
    Ans: C   Page: 524-525

32. What type of ore deposits form where minerals precipitate from fluids along the walls of faults and joints?
    A) disseminated deposits   C) sedimentary deposits
    B) placer deposits   D) vein deposits
    Ans: D   Page: 526

33. Which of the following type of ore deposits are disseminated deposits?
    A) banded iron deposits of the Great Lakes region
    B) coal deposits of the Appalachian Mountains
    C) gold placer deposits of California
    D) porphyry copper deposits of the southwest United States
    Ans: D   Page: 527

34. What important metal is extracted from the large open-pit mines of the southwestern United States and Chile?
    A) copper   B) iron   C) nickel   D) zinc
    Ans: A   Page: 527

35. What ore mineral is the major source of lead?
    A) chalcopyrite   B) galena   C) pyrite   D) sphalerite
    Ans: B   Page: 527

Use the following to answer questions 36-37:

The following questions refer to the map of North America depicted below.

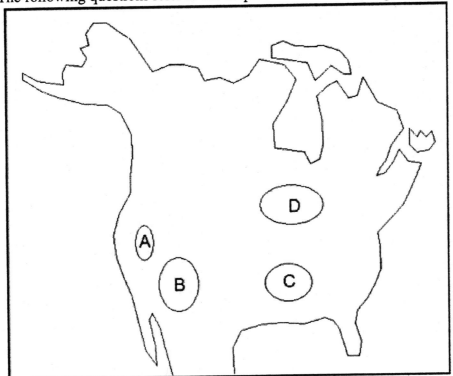

36. Large copper porphyry deposits are found in _____.
    A) region A   B) region B   C) region C   D) region D
    Ans: B   Page: 527

37. Which region provides most of the iron ore for North America?
    A) region A   B) region B   C) region C   D) region D
    Ans: D   Page: 530

38. Copper ore deposits are _____.
    A) hydrothermal ore deposits   C) sedimentary ore deposits
    B) igneous ore deposits   D) all of the above
    Ans: D   Page: 527-529

39. Which of the following metals is concentrated by crystals that settle on the floor of a
    magma chamber?
    A) gold   B) iron   C) lead   D) platinum
    Ans: D   Page: 528

40. Which of the following types of ore deposits contains rare elements, such as boron, lithium, and fluorine?
    A) ophiolites   B) pegmatites   C) placers   D) porphyry deposits
    Ans: B   Page: 528

41. Diamonds are found in _____ igneous rocks, called kimberlites, which erupt from great depth.
    A) felsic   B) intermediate   C) mafic   D) ultramafic
    Ans: D   Page: 528

42. What type of rock is required to make cement and is an important building stone?
    A) basalt   B) granite   C) limestone   D) sandstone
    Ans: C   Alternative Location: Online quizzing   Page: 529

43. When did the world's major iron ore deposits form?
    A) during the Cenozoic   C) during the Paleozoic
    B) during the Mesozoic   D) during the Precambrian
    Ans: D   Page: 529

44. Which of the following statements regarding hydrothermal ore deposits is <u>false</u>?
    A) Hydrothermal ore deposits are commonly associated with shallow granitic intrusions.
    B) Minerals precipitating from "black smokers" at mid-ocean spreading centers are an example of a modern hydrothermal ore deposit.
    C) Most hydrothermal ore deposits consist of metallic sulfides.
    D) Placers represent one type of hydrothermal ore deposit.
    Ans: D   Page: 530

45. What type of ore deposits have been concentrated by the mechanical sorting action of river currents?
    A) disseminated ore deposits   C) igneous ore deposits
    B) hydrothermal ore deposits   D) placer deposits
    Ans: D   Page: 530

46. The copper ore deposits of Cyprus, which played an important role in the economy of ancient Greece, formed _____.
    A) at a convergent plate boundary   C) at a transform plate boundary
    B) at a divergent plate boundary   D) in an intraplate setting
    Ans: B   Page: 531

Use the following to answer questions 47-49:

The following questions refer to the schematic cross section below.

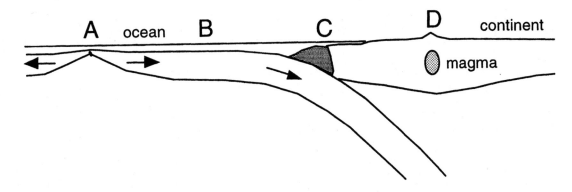

47. In what plate tectonic setting are copper porphyry deposits located?
    A) plate tectonic setting A   C) plate tectonic setting C
    B) plate tectonic setting B   D) plate tectonic setting D
    Ans: D   Page: 531-532

48. Rich copper-, lead-, and zinc-sulfide deposits, like those of Cyprus, form in which plate tectonic setting?
    A) plate tectonic setting A   C) plate tectonic setting C
    B) plate tectonic setting B   D) plate tectonic setting D
    Ans: A   Page: 531-532

49. Manganese nodules form in which region?
    A) plate tectonic setting A   C) plate tectonic setting C
    B) plate tectonic setting B   D) plate tectonic setting D
    Ans: B   Page: 531-532

50. Nodules rich in _____ are found on the deep sea floor away from plate boundaries.
    A) aluminum   B) gold   C) manganese   D) potassium
    Ans: C   Page: 531-532

Chapter 23: Earth's Environment, Global Change, and Human Impacts

1. What is the current population of Earth?
   A) about 1 billion   B) about 3 billion   C) about 6 billion   D) about 12 billion
   Ans: C   Page: 541

2. Which of the following statements is <u>true</u>?
   A) Energy use is increasing four times faster than the Earth's population.
   B) Energy use is increasing two times faster than the Earth's population.
   C) Energy use and the Earth's population are increasing at the same rate.
   D) The Earth's population is increasing two times faster than energy use.
   Ans: B   Page: 541

3. How has the concentration of carbon dioxide in the atmosphere changed since the start
   of the Industrial Revolution?
   A) Carbon dioxide concentrations have increased 3%.
   B) Carbon dioxide concentrations have increased 10%.
   C) Carbon dioxide concentrations have increased 30%.
   D) Carbon dioxide concentrations have increased 100%.
   Ans: C   Page: 542

4. Approximately how long does it take for a parcel of air to circle the globe?
   A) about a day   B) about a week   C) about a month   D) about a year
   Ans: C   Page: 544

5. Which of the following processes produces ozone?
   A) absorption of infrared radiation   C) ionization by ultraviolet radiation
   B) chemical weathering   D) photosynthesis
   Ans: C   Page: 545

6. What is the cryosphere?
   A) barren desert   C) upper atmosphere
   B) ice caps and glaciers   D) upper mantle beneath the lithosphere
   Ans: B   Page: 545

7. Which of the following is <u>not</u> a greenhouse gas?
   A) carbon dioxide   B) methane   C) sulfur dioxide   D) water vapor
   Ans: C   Page: 545, 549

8. Which of the following statements about large volcanic eruptions, such as the 1991 eruption of Mt. Pinatubo, is <u>true</u>?
   A) Global temperatures decrease and return to normal in about two weeks.
   B) Global temperatures decrease and return to normal in about four years.
   C) Global temperatures increase and return to normal in about two weeks.
   D) Global temperatures increase and return to normal in about four years.
   Ans: B   Page: 546

9. Compared to the visible part of the electromagnetic spectrum, infrared radiation has
   _____.
   A) longer wavelengths and higher   C) shorter wavelengths and higher
      energies   energies
   B) longer wavelengths and lower energies D) shorter wavelengths and lower
                                              energies
   Ans: B   Page: 546

10. What is the Earth's albedo?
    A) the fraction of Earth's surface that is covered by land
    B) the fraction of Earth's surface that is covered by oceans
    C) the fraction of solar energy absorbed by the Earth's surface
    D) the fraction of solar energy reflected by the Earth's surface
    Ans: D   Page: 546

11. Which of the following occurs with increasing temperature?
    A) The energy radiated by a black body decreases and the wavelength decreases.
    B) The energy radiated by a black body decreases and the wavelength increases.
    C) The energy radiated by a black body increases and the wavelength decreases.
    D) The energy radiated by a black body increases and the wavelength increases.
    Ans: C   Page: 546-547

12. If Earth's atmosphere did <u>not</u> contain greenhouse gases, the Earth's surface would be
    _____.
    A) approximately 33 °C cooler   C) approximately 10 °C warmer
    B) approximately 10 °C cooler   D) approximately 33 °C warmer
    Ans: A   Page: 547

13. Which of the following statements is <u>true</u>?
    A) Negative and positive feedbacks <u>both</u> tend to amplify changes in a system.
    B) Negative feedbacks tend to amplify changes in a system; positive feedbacks tend to stabilize a system.
    C) Negative feedbacks tend to stabilize a system; positive feedbacks tend to amplify changes in a system.
    D) Negative and positive feedbacks <u>both</u> tend to stabilize a system.
    Ans: C   Page: 547

14. The greenhouse effect is caused by _____.
    A) carbon dioxide and water vapor that trap heat radiating from the Earth's surface
    B) heating of homes and businesses, which releases excess heat into the atmosphere
    C) oceans that trap heat radiating from the Earth's seafloors
    D) too many plants on the surface of the Earth, which prevent cooling of the surface
    Ans: A   Page: 547

15. Solar radiation absorbed by the Earth's ground surface is reemitted as _____.
    A) infrared radiation   C) visible radiation
    B) ultraviolet radiation   D) x-ray radiation
    Ans: A   Page: 547

16. The amount of energy input to the Earth's surface is _____ the heat flowing out of the Earth's deep interior.
    A) much greater than   C) slightly less than
    B) slightly greater than   D) much less than
    Ans: A   Page: 547

17. Which of the following is a negative feedback within the climate system?
    A) albedo
    B) radiation
    C) water vapor
    D) none of the above (all are positive feedbacks)
    Ans: B   Page: 548

18. What is Earth's albedo?
    A) approximately 10%   C) approximately 60%
    B) approximately 30%   D) approximately 90%
    Ans: B   Page: 548

19. Which of the following energy fluxes is the greatest?
    A) energy flowing out of the Earth's interior
    B) solar energy absorbed by Earth's atmosphere
    C) solar energy absorbed by Earth's surface
    D) solar energy reflected by clouds and surface
    Ans: C   Page: 548

20. Which of the following climate feedback systems is considerably uncertain in that we do not know whether the net effect is a positive feedback or a negative feedback?
    A) albedo   B) clouds   C) plant growth   D) water vapor
    Ans: B   Page: 548-549

21. Which of the following is <u>not</u> a fundamental law of physics?
    A) conservation of density   C) conservation of mass
    B) conservation of energy   D) conservation of momentum
    Ans: A   Page: 549

22. Chemical analysis of ice cores demonstrates that as temperature increases, concentrations of atmospheric _____.
    A) carbon dioxide and methane <u>both</u> decrease
    B) carbon dioxide decreases while methane increases
    C) carbon dioxide increases while methane decreases
    D) carbon dioxide and methane <u>both</u> increase
    Ans: D   Page: 550

23. Which of the following is the current warm interglacial period?
    A) Holocene   B) Miocene   C) Paleocene   D) Pleistocene
    Ans: A   Page: 550

24. Based on ice core data, how rapidly can Earth shift from glacial to interglacial temperatures?
    A) 10 to 30 years   C) 1000 to 3000 years
    B) 100 to 300 years   D) 10,000 to 30,000 years
    Ans: A   Page: 550

25. How often do El Niño events occur?
    A) roughly every 5 years   C) roughly every 100 years
    B) roughly every 20 years   D) roughly every 400 years
    Ans: A   Page: 551

26. How much did the average surface temperature increase during the twentieth century?
    A) approximately 0.3 °C   C) approximately 1.2 °C
    B) approximately 0.6 °C   D) approximately 2.4 °C
    Ans: B   Page: 551

27. During an El Niño year, which of the following occurs?
    A) The Pacific trade winds decrease and cool water accumulates in the eastern Pacific.
    B) The Pacific trade winds decrease and warm water accumulates in the eastern Pacific.
    C) The Pacific trade winds increase and cool water accumulates in the eastern Pacific.
    D) The Pacific trade winds increase and warm water accumulates in the eastern Pacific.
    Ans: B   Page: 552-553

28. The residence time of sodium in the ocean is approximately _____ years.
    A) 400   B) 20,000   C) 1 million   D) 50 million
    Ans: D   Page: 554

29. Which of the following elements has the longest residence time in the atmosphere?
    A) nitrogen
    B) oxygen
    C) sulfur dioxide
    D) Nitrogen, oxygen, and sulfur dioxide <u>all</u> have the same residence time.
    Ans: A   Page: 554

30. Which of the following elements has the shortest residence time in the oceans?
    A) calcium
    B) iron
    C) sodium
    D) Calcium, iron, and sodium <u>all</u> have the same residence time.
    Ans: B   Page: 554-556

31. Which of the following carbon fluxes is the <u>greatest</u>?
    A) air-sea gas exchange   C) photosynthesis and respiration
    B) chemical weathering   D) volcanism
    Ans: C   Page: 556

32. Which of the following processes removes carbon from the atmosphere?
    A) photosynthesis   B) respiration   C) volcanism   D) all of the above
    Ans: A   Page: 556

33. Weathering of carbonate and silicate rocks _____.
    A) adds carbon to the atmosphere and the lithosphere
    B) adds carbon to the atmosphere and removes carbon from the lithosphere
    C) removes carbon from the atmosphere and adds carbon to the lithosphere
    D) removes carbon from the atmosphere and the lithosphere
    Ans: D   Page: 556-557

34. What proportion of the total amount of carbon dioxide emitted into the atmosphere each year stays in the atmosphere?
    A) approximately 25%   C) approximately 75%
    B) approximately 50%   D) approximately 100%
    Ans: B   Page: 557

35. Which of the following has dramatically changed the carbon cycle over the past 150 years?
    A) burial of organic carbon   C) deposition of carbon-rich sediments
    B) burning of fossil fuels   D) volcanism
    Ans: B   Page: 557

36. Sulfur dioxide is emitted from power plants that burn coal containing large amounts of the mineral _____.
   A) biotite   B) hematite   C) muscovite   D) pyrite
   Ans: D   Page: 558

37. Which of the following is responsible for most acid rain?
   A) automobiles
   B) chlorofluorocarbons
   C) coal-burning power plants
   D) volcanoes
   Ans: C   Page: 558

38. Acid rain is composed of _____ acids.
   A) hydrochloric and nitric
   B) oxalic and hydrochloric
   C) sulfuric and nitric
   D) sulfuric and oxalic
   Ans: C   Page: 558-559

39. Solar radiation transforms oxygen molecules in the upper atmosphere into which of the following compounds?
   A) carbon dioxide   B) chlorine   C) ozone   D) water vapor
   Ans: C   Page: 560

40. Which area in the United States has the most acidic rain?
   A) northwest U.S.   B) southwest U.S.   C) northeast U.S.   D) southeast U.S.
   Ans: C   Page: 560

41. What is the chemical formula for ozone?
   A) O   B) O_2 C) O_3 D) O_4
   Ans: C   Page: 560

42. Which of the following statements regarding ozone is <u>false</u>?
   A) Chlorofluorocarbons are depleting the ozone layer.
   B) Ozone absorbs harmful infrared radiation.
   C) Ozone forms from oxygen in the stratosphere.
   D) Ozone is a greenhouse gas.
   Ans: B   Page: 560

43. Excessive exposure to UV (ultraviolet) radiation can cause _____.
   A) cataracts   B) reduced crop yields   C) skin cancer   D) <u>all</u> of the above
   Ans: D   Page: 560

44. Which of the following treaties phased out CFC (chlorofluorocarbon) production?
   A) Geneva Accord
   B) Kyoto Treaty
   C) Montreal Protocol
   D) Vienna Agreement
   Ans: B   Page: 560

45. When sunlight reacts with CFCs (chlorofluorocarbons), _____ is released.
    A) chlorine   B) methane   C) ozone   D) sulfur dioxide
    Ans: A   Page: 560

46. In 1985, a large hole in the ozone layer was found over _____.
    A) Antarctica   B) Brazil   C) the North Pole   D) Siberia
    Ans: A   Page: 560

47. By the end of the next century temperatures are predicted to rise _____ because of global warming.
    A) less than 1.5 °C   B) 1.5 to 6 °C   C) 6 to 20 °C   D) greater than 20 °C
    Ans: B   Page: 561

48. Over the next century the warming and expanding of oceans due to global warming would result in a rise in sea level of as much as _____.
    A) 90 centimeters   B) 9 meters   C) 90 meters   D) 900 meters
    Ans: A   Page: 562

49. If all human activities that generated carbon dioxide were to stop, how long would it take for atmospheric carbon dioxide to return to its preindustrial level?
    A) 2 months   B) 2 years   C) 20 years   D) 200 years
    Ans: D   Page: 562

50. Which of the following will not reduce the emissions of greenhouse gases?
    A) using coal rather than oil and gasoline
    B) using energy more efficiently
    C) using fuel made from renewable resources such as wind
    D) using nuclear power redesigned for safety
    Ans: A   Page: 563